W9-BNT-831

EMBRACING DEMENTIA

A Call to Love
♥♥

Ellen Marie Edmonds
Mother, Grandmother, Godmother, Widow

Copyright © 2008
Ellen Marie Edmonds

First Edition -- October 7, 2008

Cover Artwork: "joyful" by Brantley

All rights reserved.
No part of the book may be used or reproduced
In any manner whatsoever
Without written permission of the author

All references to Holy Scripture are from the New Revised Standard Version
(NRSV) Catholic Edition Anglicized Text, unless otherwise noted.

PUBLISHED 2008 BY:

DeetBrari, LLC ♥♥
5184 Caldwell Mill Road
Suite 204-255
Birmingham, Alabama 35244

ISBN: 978-0-9821984-1-4

Regular Print Edition

ABOUT THE COVER ARTWORK
"Joyful" by Brantley

The cover artwork entitled "Joyful" is a water color painted in 2007 by the author's granddaughter, Brantley, who was 3-years old at the time. Brantley is quite gifted in many forms of artwork, and is especially drawn to water color and pen painting.

For the first three years of Brantley's life, she had spent four days a week with her grandmother, whom she named "Deet." At 2-years of age, she had begun attending a Mothers' Day Out program at The Adventure Nook. When her piece "Joyful" was painted, Brantley was 3 years old and had just begun fulltime attendance at Our Lady of Sorrows preschool. The change from "Deet Days" was a challenging transition for both Brantley and Deet, who had grown quite attached to each other. While Deet was experiencing the "omega" journey of her husband's vascular dementia and death, Brantley had been her "alpha" of hope.

Brantley and Deet missed each other very much. Then one day Deet asked Brantley if she would like to have a "Deet Day" and skip school...and Brantley exclaimed a heartfelt "YES!"

On the way to Deet's house, Brantley's little legs were joyfully swinging from her car seat. "Deeeeeet!" she said excitedly. "When we get to your house, I want to paint a picture for you!" "That would be lovely!" Deet said. And in her room, Brantley sat at her table with a blank sheet of paper, water paints, water bowls, and paper towels. About an hour later, she called out, "Deeeeeet! I'm finished." And there it was. In awe, Deet said, "Brantley that is *beautiful!* Thank you so much!" Then the artist Brantley grabbed her brush and said, "Wait...." And dabbing a little red paint, she proclaimed, "There, it's finished!"

Clearly, Brantley's masterpiece expressed the joy of both their hearts. And as the background for this book's cover, "Joyful" mysteriously reveals - to the seeking heart - the joy of life hidden behind the cloudy veil of dementia.

Dedicated to Frank
And all our Little Friends
Who are teaching me
How to Love

♥♥

St. Paul - teacher of love - Pray for us!

Eternal rest grant unto Frank, oh Lord; let perpetual light shine upon him; May his soul and the souls of all the faithful departed, through the mercy of God, Rest in peace. Amen

CONTENTS

Preface by Father Angelus Shaughnessy, O.F.M. Cap.   11

Introduction by Ellen Marie Edmonds   17

A Frank Commentary   21

Acknowledgments   23

Chapter 1   Our Story   25

Chapter 2   Signs of Change   51

Chapter 3   The New Reality   67

Chapter 4   Embracing the Truth   75

Chapter 5   Faith, Hope, and Forgiveness   83

Chapter 6   Spiritual Direction   95

Chapter 7   The Call to Love   105

Chapter 8   Pain and Darkness   127

Chapter 9   Grief the Thief   133

Chapter 10   Humor the Healer   147

Chapter 11   Family, Friends, and My Journal   155

Chapter 12   Help! Searching for Sitters   161

Chapter 13   "The Club"   165

Chapter 14   The Angel Miss Mawbley   185

Chapter 15   Home Again!   189

Chapter 16   Hospice and Hope   193

Chapter 17   Living the Present Moment *In a Nutshell*   197

Chapter 18   Giving Joy, Finding Joy: New Ways to Celebrate   215

Chapter 19   Letting Go and Giving Permission   221

Chapter 20   Frank's First Christmas   225

Chapter 21   Celebrating Death - Remembering Life   231

After Word by Ellen Marie Edmonds   235

References   238

Index of Poems   239

Preface

Father Angelus Shaughnessy, O.F.M. Cap.

Why This Book

As Ellen's spiritual director for several years, and throughout her husband's illness, I often observed the strength of her faith through her sobs of tears as she lost her husband and best friend to dementia, one inch at a time. She would come frequently to Holy Mass and to receive the sacraments. Clearly, it was her faith, hope and love which sustained, nurtured, and transformed them. During a spiritual direction session a few months after Frank's death, Ellen shared with me some of her journal entries and confessed how she had been transformed through this journey of unconditional love. Then I asked her, "What is it you have to do for God, Ellen, before you can die?" She responded that she believed she is called to share with others, as a sign of hope and courage, how God revealed Himself and His love through this experience, and how she responded to this life-altering season. Thus, this book is the story of two souls united by God in their hearts, their bodies, and their crosses on their life journey together.

Each soul is created by God with a purpose of being. To each soul, God gives a heart and body with a purpose of loving. Thus, every human is created - and fully equipped - by God, for a purpose known only to His will and fulfilled through the searching, finding, and accepting of this Knowing. This "knowing" is the intimate love of the Creator for His creature. And Holy Scripture tells us that whoever asks and seeks God's will, finds it. "My sheep know me, and they hear my voice, " Jesus tells us.

Acceptance of God's will is, perhaps, the single most important ingredient of finding peace in this life on earth. It has been said that from the moment of conception, life is a series of losses and response to losses. When one embraces this reality of life and seeks God's will to find purpose and meaning, the human experience becomes an adventure with the Divine in faith, hope, and love. The brilliance of God's light shines forth in the darkest night, perhaps giving darkness its greatest purpose. There is where the soul is infused with a spring time of God's love and Knowing.

C. S. Lewis in his book, *A Grief Observed,* describes the pain of a lost loved one as feeling a lot like fear. We know that God is love. We know He loves us. When we love and are loved by another human, we know this love is God's presence with us. When a loved one dies, whether from dementia and/or from physical death, there is terrible pain. The pain of such loss exists only because we have known love. Accordingly, we can say that where pain is present, love is present, God is present. God is with us in our pain. When we realize this, and accept that this pain is the sacrifice of love, we can better understand what Jesus means when He says, "If you love me, pick up *your* cross and follow me." *Your* cross. It is the unique journey of discovering God, His love, His will for you which He has designed only for *you*. Realizing that God is present with us through the losses and pain of life, and accepting that His will prevails (whether ordained or allowed), is the way of picking up *your* cross and finding peace in its splinters and when we fall. Remember, even Jesus - fully human *and* fully divine - fell three times carrying His cross. He expects that we - who are *not* fully divine - will fall with our cross. And so, He promises always to be there with us, to help carry it and to help us up when we fall. Always.

This thing called "dementia." An experience of the darkest night, some might say. And yet, we know that light is brighter when darkness is darker. Could it be that God has allowed the dark plague of dementia, in all its forms throughout the world, to help us see the light of His Love? When "all is well" do we seek and find Him? Could it be that even in this seemingly tragic experience, His mercy and love are guiding us?

Ellen's love for God and for her husband, combined with her strong faith and hope, enabled her to fully embrace her husband's illness and to companion him in the commitment of compassionate love. It is truly a story of faith, hope, and unconditional love.

-Father Angelus Shaughnessy, OFM Cap.

Father Angelus Shaughnessy, Order of Friars Minor Capuchin, has been a Catholic priest for over 53 years and is a world renown speaker, writer, teacher, and retreat master. After circling the globe four times in ministry service, Father Angelus spent six years at Eternal Word Television Network (EWTN) in Birmingham, Alabama serving as Minister General to the Franciscan Missionaries of the Eternal Word, where he regularly preached via television to millions worldwide. At the present time, Father Angelus is serving as the National Executive Director of the Archconfraternity of Christian Mothers in Pittsburgh, Pennsylvania.

TRANSFORMED

When you were on top of your Cherokee mountain
You invited me into your heart
I said "yes"
And life was so very, very good…

We savored the fruits on top of the mountain
Love, faith, hope and good health
Family, friends – strangers, too
We loved and enjoyed them together

In the night like a thief our cross did come
On the crest of the Indians' mountain
A car from behind – a blow to your head
Sent our life, our hearts
Down your mountain

Sage to adolescent to toddler to babe
Inch by inch – all the way down
To the base of your mountain where life began
And where awaited your glorious crown
Loving you, holding you, being with you
Together – down, down, down

It was Christmastime and Heaven's choir
Sang, "Please Come Home for Christmas"
I said to you, "You're about to go home
Well done – good and faithful servant!"
I rested my head upon your shoulder
Jesus – upon your heart
The good-bye beat, your PhD
Your passion: you did your part
And Jesus changed this sheep's heart.

"Unless you become as a little child
You can't enter the Kingdom of Heaven"
"Whatsoever you do to the least of My brothers
That you do unto Me"
"When I was sick, you comforted Me…"

Thank you, Lord, for letting me love You
Christmastime – Gift – Crown
Father God on top of the mountain
Baby Jesus, all the way down

©Ellen Marie Edmonds 2008

Introduction
Ellen Marie Edmonds

Dementia is a heart-wrenching brain disease which plagues modern society worldwide. Whether manifesting as vascular dementia, or Alzheimer's disease, or some other form, dementia often appears as a thief in the night which robs its host of mental, cognitive, and physical life. Everyone today knows someone affected by this disease. Our relationship to the victim of dementia directly determines the impact the disease will have on us - and consequently, how we respond to it. And the greater the sphere of influence the afflicted person has had, the greater the sphere of impact will be. When the victim is one's spouse, parent, child, or sibling there is a special call to sacrificial love and life adjustments.

This book is the story of my personal faith journey embracing my husband's vascular dementia disease which was triggered by a head injury he sustained in an automobile accident. As the patriarch of a large family, and as a prominent figure in various areas of corporate, military, political, and community life, he maintained numerous unique relationships which were all affected in some way by his disease. As his spouse, the primary impact and response was mine.

One of the greatest difficulties I encountered in our journey with vascular dementia was the lack of education and resources available to me and to others walking my path. There just did not seem to be any dependable support groups available, little or no understanding of the profound grief that my husband was experiencing - and that I was experiencing, and limited availability of care facilities and services for people with dementia. The one thing I did have was a great capacity to love, and as my husband always said "a lot of resilience to life's blows." This is my story of how life was, how it was tragically changed by an accident and dementia, how I responded, and what God taught me. Told within the framework of my own simple and strong faith - while respecting the faith and philosophies of others, this story of our journey through dementia provides helpful knowledge, practical tools, and hope for anyone affected by the disease.

As I've grown older and survived many life difficulties, a very strong faith in God and the sureness of His promises provided an abundance of hope which has kept me going. Even today, I embrace the darkness of dusk and find hope in each new sunrise. And He has taught me that every ending has a beginning, because He is the Alpha and the Omega. True to His word, He sent my first granddaughter, Brantley Elizabeth, at the onset of my husband's dementia. She was and is a beautiful reminder of life, love, and hope. And on the day my husband was dying, we learned that my precious daughter, Shayne, was pregnant and expecting my second grand-daughter, Riley Briel - our little songbird! Alpha with the Omega! God is good, and He always provides - if we will but be still - and watch in faith with the eyes and ears of our hearts.

There were so many surprises on this journey, particularly the responses of family and friends to Frank's changes. Many, many friends became our family and surrounded us with loving support. Many disappeared, never to return. Always, as I encountered and responded to daily challenges, I prayed and shared my responses with family, friends, my spiritual director

Father Angelus Shaughnessy, or our spiritual companion Father Palmer, and oftentimes with complete strangers. At times, *anyone* who would listen and be present with me was an angel sent by God.

Several times over the years I was asked to write about my experiences to help people struggling with spousal or parental dementia. My brother Richard suggested that I teach those in facilities and with sitter services who care for the demented; and my friend Lynn suggested I teach others through church seminars and the media. A hospice nurse I met in Alaska asked if I would write for hospice staff and families. Finally, at the urging (three times!) of my spiritual director Father Angelus and the affirmation of my bishop, Robert Baker, Diocese of Birmingham, I completed this book which had its inception in the poetry and journals I wrote during the last year of Frank's life. The journal writing that reflected the raw experience of my daily encounter with dementia would become the source of my new understanding of how God was manifesting His will in our lives.

For those with little time to read or who need immediate help in their care for someone with advanced dementia, hospice care for dementia, or any other terminal disease, it might be particularly beneficial to first read Chapter 17, *Living the Present Moment* and its section "In A Nutshell."

It is my hope that all who hear or read our story will find practical help in the technical experiences (how I managed the changes, etc.) and also be encouraged in faith and hope. The key word in my story is *embracing* dementia. My prayer is that all who are facing this challenge will embrace in truth what is happening, and then prepare themselves in faith and acceptance for a glorious ride backwards into the unknown, to find in their loved one the same Christ child Who teaches us that hidden in love are the mysteries of eternal life.

A *Frank* Commentary

"Frank Edmonds was always involved in things that are good." Those were the words spoken to me recently by a Boy Scout executive with the Andrew Jackson Council in Jackson, Mississippi. How true those words! This was a man who loved God and country, loved his family, loved friends and strangers, loved children, animals, and especially nature. "Frank Edmonds the Man: family man, church man, telephone man, soldier; scouter, banker, mediator, board member, and civic leader; he did it all. He was not afraid of sacrifice or to fight for whom or what he believed in; nor would he support something he did *not* believe in. I knew him as a strong and gentle giant, full of great wisdom and compassion. As a man who engaged life to the fullest, he sought to make things better than he found them. His heart and gift were especially drawn to the less fortunate in life and to recognizing and helping little people of all color and creed.

Although Frank's career life was dedicated to the telecommunications industry as an AT&T corporate officer, he was most proud of having been a World War II veteran. "I'm just a soldier," he would tell me during his latter days. Defending his country for the God he believed in and the people he loved came first. That spirit of protective sacrifice was part of his make-up that surfaced throughout his life. When he was asked to serve our country as Civilian Aide to the Secretary of the Army, a civilian post which carries the protocol of a 3-star general, Frank Edmonds responded in that same honorable spirit. Time after time, he accepted leadership roles in numerous church and community organizations that helped society.

As a board member of The Piney Woods Country Life School in Mississippi, one of four remaining African-American boarding schools in the country, Frank was honored to help underprivileged boys and girls, in a faith environment, become successful leaders in their fields.

Serving the Boy Scouts of America as a registered scout and in council leadership for over 65 years, Frank was honored with the Silver Beaver Award and the "N. Frank Edmonds 1982 Class of Eagle Scouts." And posthumously, Frank was honored with the rare Golden Eagle award.

How blessed and proud I am to have been chosen to be his wife, to have witnessed his contribution to the world; blessed indeed.

If Frank Edmonds could say one thing *today* about our journey of *yesterday*, it would be that he would suffer through it all over again if others could learn from and be helped by his experience, and if one soul could be saved by learning what it really means to love. Thank you, Frank - I love you, too. And what a lovely dance it is…

Acknowledgments

Many wonderful people – too many to name - were there for us during this journey. Frank would join me in thanking the following special people who loved us and supported us before, during, and after his illness. This was a family cross, and we all needed each other. For each of you I offer prayer of gratitude, and I beg Heaven that, if your own life or the life of someone you love, presents the cross of dementia or another life changing illness, you will be blessed with the presence and the sacrificial gift of love from people who care for you as you have cared for Frank and me. I gratefully and humbly thank God for you.

My daughter Shayne and her family: Clay, Brantley, & Riley
My siblings: Barbara, Steve (RIP), Richard, & Susan

My Aunt Alice

My Thirteen Godchildren

Special Sisters: Beverly, Barbara, Lynn, Dawn, Janice, Peggy, Lenore & Sharon
Special Brothers: Al (RIP), Denny, Jack, & Jim
Angels: Cary, Jimmy, Brenton, Miss Mawbley, Bob, & Maureen,
Father Angelus Shaughnessy, O.F.M. Cap., my spiritual director
Father Palmer, our spiritual companion and my journal advisor
Many Other Special Family Priests
Mother Angelica, the Poor Clare Nuns, and the priests and brothers of
The Franciscan Missionaries of the Eternal Word (EWTN)

Our AT&T/BellSouth Retired Officers Family
The United States Army
The Arlington Ladies and the Staff of Arlington National Cemetery
Boy Scouts of America, Andrew Jackson Council
Community Grief Support Services
Our Lady of the Valley Church Grief Support

* * * * * * * * * * * * * * * * * * * *

CHAPTER
ONE

♥♥

Circles in the Wind...

Two tiny bubbles
Of Love, of Life
Spoken in the Breath
Of God Himself
Different time, different season
Different purpose and reason
Drawn together...
Circles in the Wind

Came the widower late
To my heart's gate
Lonely circles...
Enjoined by the Wind

The price He paid for Love was death
The price we pay – the same
Had we not shared
The cross of pain
Our circles would have joined in vain
Empty bubbles, bursting in the wind
Nay, Heaven's our path, our goal our gain
Grace filled...
Circles in the Wind

In His will we grew
In His will we blew
Chosen circles in the Wind
Living and giving
All that we had
Weeping...
Circles in the Wind

Alpha and Omega
One and the Same
No start no end – one moment
Here or there our hearts still share
His gift of our Sacred Moment
Eternal...
Circles in the Wind

©Ellen Marie Edmonds 2008

Chapter 1: **Our Story**

Whenever two hearts meet in life, each comes with its history of loving and of being loved, which eternally shapes the heart in its capacity to love. The more one knows about another's heart, the more is known of the person's history. I affectionately refer to that history as the "heartstory." Frank and I were blessed with sixteen love-filled years of marriage. He had his story. I had my story. Together, we wrote our story.

Both of us as children had lost our fathers to sudden death. Our mothers had been sick and/or absent most of our lives. Life had forced each of us to grow up well before our time. Marriage and parenting had taught us the meaning of sacrificial love and its ultimate price: we both had suffered spousal loss due to death or divorce. As survivors of adversity, we shared similar strengths and values, and also complimentary differences. The brief account I give of *his* story is about the man I knew and loved as my husband of sixteen years, whose life I was privileged to witness and contribute to; it is also based upon his many personal testimonies to me, and those of others who knew and loved him. For obvious reasons, my *own* story is more detailed, and describes life events which I believe prepared me for the story Frank and I would ultimately write together.

Frank was an only child and, after his father's death, was raised by his maternal grandparents. His grandfather, a Methodist minister, died fairly young, leaving only "Big Mama" in Frank's life. Her faith was very strong. Having been raised Catholic, she taught Frank the faith she knew and invaluable life lessons, which he often recalled to me. At 17, he lost Big Mama, but not before she gave him the precious gift of hope in the words, "Junior, you'll be fine. You can do anything you want to do." His friend, Mack, found him crying behind the barn and invited him to live with him and his wife, who was Frank's cousin. Mack also gave Frank his first job, delivering ice. A very creative soul, Frank developed into quite the entrepreneur as he learned to survive. He married, went to war, and experienced the painful loss of fellow soldiers. Upon returning to the states, he completed his degree in Physics from Vanderbilt's Peabody College, and began a successful telephone career which landed him the CEO position. But in his worldly successes, he never forgot his roots; and that sweet sense of humility, I believe, was the reason he was so successful. I must confess, however, that I married him in the evening of life. Though I did not personally know him in his early years of managing family, career, and life issues, the man I tell you about is the man I married, whose life I was blessed to witness.

My story is a different shade of purple. As a child survivor of many tragedies, I share details to help those struggling with life's obstacles, and particularly to give hope to those facing dementia. Faith in adversity can shape and strengthen us when heroic love calls. Frank recognized that characteristic in me the first time we met. I was a strong woman with a simple and strong faith; my story tells why.

We were a military family. When I was born, my father was away at war. At 2 years of age, shortly after Dad came home, I became an orphan when Mom was sick and hospitalized for several months. Dad was working, I lived with various unfamiliar relatives; and my 8-year old brother lived in a foster home. At the ripe age of 2, my mom was gone, my "new" dad was gone, my brother was gone – and I was with strangers. In retrospect, I must have received a lot of love from my Aunt Alice (who still calls me her little brown-eyed niece!) and other relatives, because this situation could have been very traumatic to a toddler. One day, the family returned; and life went on. Dad's military career brought frequent moves, schools, and associated adjustments. At 11, I learned Dad was very sick with something called "complications" from heart disease and diabetes, so he retired from the military. Mom was 40 and expecting. Hospitalized early with complications, Mom discovered there were twins, which resulted in a seven-week premature delivery. One twin, my sister Sally, died at birth. The other twin, Susan, weighed only 3 pounds, and was hospitalized for a month. I remember Sally's funeral, and her tiny little pink brocade casket. With Dad sick and retired, Mom's situation, hospital and funeral expenses, it was a very difficult time for our family. Truly, little Susan was the light and joy of our lives. I was very proud of my baby sister; the day she came home from the hospital, I took her around and showed her to all our neighbors. Before long, it was trips to the park in her stroller, riding her in the basket of my bicycle (we did those things back then!), and taking her to all my softball games where she was the "Lucky 7's" mascot. I was the middle kid, with an older brother and sister and a younger brother and sister. One Sunday when I was 16, Dad took me to the cemetery and told me he could die soon, that Mom did not want to talk about it and that I would have to be in charge. The words were spoken, but all children believe their parents are immortal... Two months later, it happened - a heart attack came like a thief in the night. And at 16, I was in charge. Four months later, Hurricane Camille hit, destroying the entire coast, every landmark I had grown up with, and my school. The thief took my baby sister, my dad's life - - and my childhood.

Looking back, I realize that it was my dad's love and belief in me, and his teaching of fundamental truths, which equipped me for the colorful life God had designed for me. Dad once said, "It's important that you learn early in life to see the glass half full. Otherwise, you'll see everything in life from a negative view." This was an amazingly powerful life tool, which I employ over and over again to bring light to darkness and hope to despair. My brother Steve, who himself was an optimist, once told me, "You and I both know that if we find ourselves surrounded by manure, start shoveling; there must be a horse here somewhere!" Dad's point exactly. I remember telling Dad when I was about 15 that I was never getting married, because married people are always yelling and making everyone around them miserable. He wisely responded, "Your mom and I love each other very much, and we don't mean to hurt each other. We both realize it's our way of releasing frustrations, so we don't take it personally." I was glad the discussion occurred, because *I* sure took the yelling personally! Dad's explanation changed my mind about marriage, but not about their "yelling therapy"; I still prefer quiet talk… and a hug.

The next decade of my life took me on a journey of marriage, graduation, embarking on a 30-year career in telecommunications, going to college at night, and the birth of my daughter, Shayne. Ah, motherhood! Little did I know, this would be my greatest joy, my greatest learning experience, and my greatest call to sacrificial love. This would also be how I learned to understand and forgive my parents and myself, and to ask my parents and my daughter to forgive me for my own imperfections. It was how I would learn – and am still learning – about unconditional love. But what I remember most is that it's how I learned the meaning of "embracing."

That beautiful moment, when I first saw my baby girl... those were the days of mystery, when the surprise of God's gift was reserved for the birthday. I had so hoped for a little girl, but all the wise women and even the doctors predicted a boy. When God surprised me with my little girl, how providential it was that I had chosen the Irish name "Shayne" which means "gift from God." And when Dr. Gaddy handed her to me, she tucked her little arms against my heart, with her tiny birth-marked hands back-to-back as in my womb. I held her, she snuggled, and I cried. To this day, this is the way we hug each other – standing up, of course...but with her arms tucked, hands back to back, embraced by the arms and heart of her mother holding her baby. The power of love which transfers in that moment is indescribably awesome, and is often depicted in images of the Madonna and Child. If you want to be refreshed by the love of God, hold a baby close to your heart and savor the sacred moment.

It occurred to me one day, while rocking my granddaughter and pondering the infinite love of God within her, that science had recently discovered that when a baby girl is in the mother's womb, the baby girl's ovaries already contain all the eggs of every child she will ever bear. Amazing! In other words, my grandbabies – as ova - were actually in my womb, too! Given the significant role these little "alphas" played in the "omega" journey of embracing my husband's dementia, I find in this mysterious

31

manifestation of God's providence a particular gift of hope for mothers of girl babies. I wonder if Mary's mother, Anne, knew that the child Jesus was once in her own womb...

Parenting is a real eye-opener – and a soul saver. I remember thinking, "Hmmm... this must be how God feels when I disobey or hurt Him..." I remember the thought process as if it were just yesterday. With all our many responsibilities of life, I still managed to go to my then 6-year old daughter's tee ball games, and my teenaged sister's PTA meetings and her basketball cheerleader tryouts, games, etc. One day it occurred to me that as a teenager I had been an all-star softball player, and that I was honored as "Most Valuable Player" one year at the season banquet. I also played varsity tennis, and had won several singles and doubles tennis tournaments with my friend Susie. Not only were my parents not present for any of my honors; they never even came to a single softball or tennis game! All of a sudden my spirit was crushed. Pain turned to anger turned to wonder. Why did that happen? Compared to today's mindset, where kids' activities often rule the lives of the family, my story seemed like abuse! However, I let my mind and heart roll back in time, and realized that when I was 14 and 15, my dad was retired with disabilities and on a limited income. Mom was working nights. There was an older sister and brother and a new grandbaby Steve, Jr. There was a younger brother and a toddler sister. My parents' buckets were completely full. There was no luxury time left for the athletic activities of their middle kid. Having reached that point of understanding, I was then able to recognize in gratitude that God had blessed me with the love and nurturing support of my best friend's parents, the Latimers, who took me to all of our ball games and yelled for me. If they yelled, "Hit a homerun, Ellen" I did it, just for them. If they yelled, "Strike her out, Ellen," I heard and tried my best. I remembered these things. And at that moment, I realized my own shortcomings, my limitations. I knew at that moment, we all do the best we can with what we have to work with. And then, I wrote a heartfelt letter to the Latimers acknowledging with deep gratitude the significant role they had played in my childhood. We remain close even today, and they never forget my birthday.

Meanwhile, my mother was severely burned and was hospitalized for several months in a military hospital, leaving the care of my 11-year-old sister and 17-year-old brother - and all of my mother's business affairs - to me. More aging came, but still - no gray hair. Susan lived with me for the next 10 years, through her college graduation. My teenaged brother, Rich, was independently blazing his own life trail... Mom was with us sporadically, when not with other family. It was Rich she was living with on that Thursday morning, when Mom went for an early walk and was struck by a car.

Mom and Rich lived on the Coast, four hours away. The doctors said she was doing fine, and she was being moved from ICU to the orthopedic ward for shoulder surgery. It was suggested we wait and come on Saturday. But when we arrived, Mom was in a coma. In the night, she had experienced heart failure and lung collapse. Poor Mama; she suffered so much. The good Father Richard had always told me, "Pray for your mother; she can't pray for herself." Indeed we prayed, and not in vain! That late June morning, we needed a priest to anoint Mom; but her parish priest was away on vacation. We called several parishes, to no avail. But, at last, at the Church of the Nativity of the Blessed Virgin Mary where I had received my First Holy Communion as a child, a little old priest answered our call. The priest asked Mom's name and asked if she was at the military hospital. We said, "Yes, Father." And there came her miracle in a thick Irish brogue. "I saw your mother yesterday, and she asked me to hear her confession and give her last rites," the priest said. That explained why Rich had said the day before, "Mom is really doing well. She said she is the happiest she has ever been in her life and that she is at peace with God." God is so good! I told my brother and sister that Mom's suffering was over, that she was in God's hands, and that we had just witnessed the greatest answer to prayer that any Catholic could ask for. She died on Tuesday, and we celebrated her miracle and her life story.

As I recall the loss of my mother, I am reminded that she taught me so much about love in the form of affection. Mom was a "snuggler" whose unique scalp massage made all fear and worry disappear! Sometimes even today, I scratch my head and find peace in remembering... By her simple example, Mom helped develop in me the inherent instincts of *motherly love*, which I in turn have been able to share with my children – and with my husband and others. Born to mother; Mary was, too.

I am reminded, too, of having learned the precious value of *family love* through my in-laws, Caro and Papa Sid, and through sweet Nondee, who was the only grandmother I ever knew. Some called her "Sunshine" – and true to her name, she was a sparkling jewel whose smiles and stories warmed and brightened our lives for many years. Memories of Nondee continue to bless me whenever I see a Christmas cactus, or when we sing "Happy Birthday to Jesus" on Christmas Eve; but mostly, I remember her smile and how she loved people.

It is, I believe, a lovely and necessary thing to stop from time to time and smell the "roses of life." The duties of life certainly burden us with its thorns; but none can overpower the ever-present fragrance of love. Seek It! Know It! Remember It! Heal in It! Ah – the sweet cycle of Hope.

Indeed there are the thorns. Those lovely years were painfully spotted by the loss of my four babies to miscarriage. Each loss was heartbreaking; but through them collectively, I learned - the hard and stubborn way - to accept God's will in my life. He obviously saw the big picture and knew my limits. As demonstrated in the following story, we learn from our mistakes of pride.

Just prior to the fourth miscarriage, I had requested special prayer to become pregnant. When I discovered I was *already* pregnant, I sincerely believed that God was going to bless us with and through this baby. When I lost the baby, I felt betrayed by God and all alone. My faith was shaken, and since it was God to whom I had always turned in trials, I was "lost as a goose" as Frank would say. So I turned to Father Richard, God bless him! He kindly explained to me that I had confused my will with God's will, and that if I felt abandoned by God, it was I who had moved. I remember saying, "Oh, I get it. God doesn't want me to have any more children." I could accept that this was His will, but that reality was in itself as painful as the miscarriages.   Why *didn't* God want me to have babies? I was not comforted. I felt like a failure at motherhood and family. My defense mechanisms kicked in, and I decided to "go career" and accept that there would be no more babies. Pregnancy for me, I decided, was like a bad case of the flu. And there were "vaccinations" for that. So my husband and I, who had practiced natural family planning throughout our marriage, decided I should have my tubes "banded" to prevent this "illness." The doctor had told me banding had the risk of coming undone by itself, and I remember saying, "Well, if it comes undone and I end up with a baby, that would be great. I'll leave it in God's hands." Father Richard had quoted the Church's position on these matters, and recommended against the procedure. But stubbornly I had said, "God knows that I am not against procreation. He knows I want children, but it's obviously not His will to give me children. If it is His will, the band will come undone." And in response to my inner pain and anger, I proceeded. Thankfully, God knew my heart and the "why" of my action. My husband and I then tried unsuccessfully to adopt a baby through Catholic Charities. The life lesson came later, having heard of many cases where mothers had experienced intermittent births and miscarriages – not over a seven-year period, as I had experienced; but still there was the mix. I wondered if that could have happened for me. Upon realizing this, I discussed the matter of tube reversal with my spiritual director, followed his direction, and reached peace in God's mercy. Years later, at the loving suggestion of a very holy priest, Father John, I named my four little ones John Mary, Joseph Marie, Mary Therese, and Elizabeth Marie. God *did* give me those children, those tiny little rosebuds who lived in my womb and then bloomed in heaven.

They got the shortcut! They continue to be a real part of my heart and my eternal life. Often, I send them hugs through my grandbabies or other babies I embrace. The sureness of their heavenly prayer for me, for their big sister Shayne, and for their nieces Brantley and Riley, is sweetly consoling.

Ironically, years later when I married Frank he was a widower with *four* children! The one child I was blessed to birth became three children. The sister I raised as my own child became three children. They do multiply! And then there are my 13 godchildren, and all of Frank's grandchildren and great grandchildren, all of whom remain in my "mother's heart." That's more than a bucketful of souls to love and pray for! God is mercifully good *and* He has a great sense of humor. His will in His time. What the omniscient God knew - what I am still learning - is that His plan for me, for each of us, is perfect. His will is *always* perfect. What I must do is patiently accept His will, and learn to live it in love.

Humility; love; truth; understanding; forgiveness; this sequence seemed to be the formula that continues even today to sustain me mentally, spiritually, emotionally, and physically. It's how I think and how I love. Actually, it is how I have survived a young life filled with so many losses: my parents, sister, brother, four babies, and now - my beloved husband. Indeed, pain "grows us up" quickly! We can sink in a pond of misery, or we can swim in the ocean of God's mercy.

The wise old Father Richard remembers... And in kindness, he smiles and says, "Amen, sister!

As I write of this particular life lesson and how it prepared me for my husband's illness, I ponder the mystery of how the God of mercy delights in our growing in His love; how we learn from the mistakes and pains of life and love; and how He uses our humility of heart to bear fruit in the alphas and omegas of life. Since that sacred "alpha moment" years ago, when I realized that my free will may have interfered with God's divine will to create new life *in His own time*, I have strapped myself with His mercy and love and made a commitment to help others. Those who despair from having had multiple miscarriages, I help to find hope. Those in crisis pregnancies I help to realize that, no matter what the circumstance of conception, when a life is conceived, it is *God's* work – His miraculous gift of a new life is hidden within the "crisis." And I also help those suffering from the guilt of past abortions to realize God's endless gifts of mercy, forgiveness, and healing which are theirs for the asking.

And since that sacred "omega moment" of seeing the little child hidden inside my husband with vascular dementia, I am committed to helping others embrace dementia as a call from God to see and love the little one within. Truly, the *unseen* human life, whether hidden in the womb of the female or hidden in the heart of the adult with dementia, is God's unique masterpiece created with a purpose in time and eternity; and it is His call to us to love *Him* by loving His hidden little one. God's will; God's time.

That was my story. Together, we wrote our story.

Frank found me in the newspaper. At the time, he was the CEO of the phone company where I worked. A news article recognized me for a professional honor I had received, and it stated that I was a long-time phone company employee. A week or so later, I received a letter from "Mr. Edmonds the CEO" congratulating and thanking me for my leadership contribution to the community. Amazing! No manager at any level had ever done such, and I had held many similar positions in the past. I decided that the next time I was in Jackson, I would visit him and thank him personally.

The day came. No appointment had been made. As I waited in the outer office, a bit of anxiety came over me as I realized where I was. "You are going to shake his hand, thank him for taking the time to make a little person count, and leave," I reminded myself. In a few minutes, the "gentle giant" graciously received me and the anxiety was gone. "Mr. Edmonds, you are the first manager at any level who ever thanked or encouraged me for my community leadership roles, and I've had many, "I had said. "Thank you for taking the time to make a little person count." He smiled and replied, "Well, Ellen, I think it's important to recognize our employees who are active in the community, and I write letters like this all the time. But you are the first person who has ever come to thank me."

There, in that moment of two acts of gratitude, our lives crossed.

Thirty minutes later, after a most inspiring visit of accolades and encouragement, I stood up to leave. Mr. Edmonds extended a handshake and said, "I appreciate your coming to see me, Eileen." In a split second I thought, "Eileen? He thinks my name is *Eileen*?" And without further thought, I replied, "It was my pleasure Mr. *Jones*." Seeing the puzzled look on his face I smiled and said, "You can call me Eileen, and I'll call you Mr. Jones!" He recovered quickly with, "Oh, I am *so* sorry - I meant *Ellen*!" Thankfully, he appreciated the humor and quick wit, and we both laughed. And amazingly, he never forgot my name again…

Ten years passed. Due to career changes, I had moved to another state. A few years later I was left single by divorce, and the marriage was later annulled by the Church. Frank had retired, and his wife of many years had died suddenly following heart surgery. His own heart was bereft at the loss of his childhood sweetheart; his children were grown and married, and he suffered terrible loneliness. It was three years later that we married. Through Frank's four grown children came ten beautiful grandchildren, four great-grandchildren; and at the time of his death, there were three "in the oven" as Frank would say. In all, God had generated 21 lives through the man Frank. The heart of his late wife lived on in our blended family life, like the living presence of an ancient, sacred tree. Often I have said that, one day when I see her in heaven, I will thank her for having trained Frank so well in the way of family love which has blessed many, many others.

When Frank and I married, he was strong and wise, full of love and joy, loved and respected by those who knew him. Family and faith were his greatest loves, and he was fascinated by the mysteries of life. Late in his life, he became Roman Catholic, drawn ultimately by the mystery of the Eucharist and transubstantiation – that sacred moment at every celebration of Mass when the "Word *becomes* Flesh" yet *appears* as bread and wine. He was blessed with excellent physical and mental health. As a retired CEO, he remained active in the fields of telecommunications and public affairs. He had been appointed Civilian Aide to the Secretary of the Army (CASA) for several consecutive terms, and then to the lifetime appointment of CASA Emeritus. Although the CASA position is a civilian post, it carries the Army protocol rank of a 3-Star General. Another particular area of commitment for Frank was The Boy Scouts of America, which had played a significant guidance role in his life as a fatherless child. He gratefully and proudly gave back to Scouting for over 65 years, even unto death.

Although I continued working several years until I could retire, we were able to travel often and live a full life together. He was not fond of "group travel" with strict schedules – unless, of course, we were going to an Alabama or Vanderbilt college football game...But he encouraged me to go on pilgrimages. For my birthday in 1995, he gifted me with a trip to the Holy Land with Father Mitch Pacwa. I remember getting lost in a gift shop at the Jerusalem Museum, and being found by Father Mitch who fortunately could speak Hebrew! "I'm looking for a lost sheep," he had told them in Hebrew. The Holy Land was like walking through the scriptures in 3-D, giving new life to the Gospels and to contemplating the life of Jesus in the rosary prayer. A whole new door opened for my spiritual life through Eternal Word Television Network (EWTN) and Mother Angelica. I became a lay Franciscan missionary and discovered a much deeper faith, which was critical to the life journey which lay ahead. The next pilgrimage was to Guadalupe in Mexico City with the lay Franciscan missionaries, where I came to know Jesus' Mother Mary as my

41

own mother, while praying the rosary for my deceased Mom on her birthday. Next, Frank gifted me with a pilgrimage to Rome to see Pope John Paul II; to Turin, Italy to see the Holy Shroud; and to the village of Medjugorje in Bosnia, where Our Lady has reportedly been appearing to six visionaries since 1981. The sequence of these journeys was quite significant to my spiritual formation, to our married life together, and ultimately enabled me - enabled us - to accept God's will and embrace the cross of love, which awaited us.

Every day together was a delight. We shared the duties, the burdens, the expenses, and the sorrows. We shared the rewards, the joys, and the blessings. And we thanked our God together. Whenever I could, I attended daily Mass, wherever we were. In Puerto Rico, I would choose a Spanish Mass, for the added cultural blessing. Frank, who was Methodist for the first several years of our marriage, often went with me to daily Mass. When we would sing an old church hymn like Amazing Grace, Frank would say, "Now, *that's* a Methodist song!" He enjoyed what I enjoyed, and vice versa; and we learned so much about life and faith by sharing our lives with each other. Sometimes it was over a meal, sometimes just sitting together in the den; always we talked and listened to each other with eagerness. It was the way to know each other's heart. It was the way to know how to please the other. It was the way of married love, complete with romance, friendship, and unconditional commitment.

There was a holy presence in our togetherness. There is a peaceful knowing that married couples experience, where nothing has to be said or done, and where the ultimate communication of love occurs. Doing nothing, together, wherever, sharing the present moment.

A particular attribute unique to Frank was his ability to quickly determine someone's strengths and gifts, after having only known and talked with them for a few minutes. It is why he was a master at the art of public affairs. But on a family level, this gift of his was instrumental, especially in my daughter's life, and in my own. He was a great encourager.

For all of Shayne's early childhood, I had been a working mom. Our time together was very precious, but never seemed to be enough. Even today regret lingers in my heart for not having had more one-on-one time, which is so important to a child's sense of security, and to the mother's heart and soul. This is something I'm still learning today, from the God of Second Chances, as I try to "get it right" in caring for my grandchildren. Fortunately, when Frank and I married, he was already retired, and a new parenting opportunity was born. The then teenaged Shayne would wake in the morning and seek Frank out in his office, and then settle into the loveseat near his chair; and together they would begin each new day with a half hour of quality time, talking and listening and growing together. With fatherly eyes and a wise heart, he reflected back to her the beauty of her being, her God-given gifts, and her unique purpose in life. After just a few months of Frank's loving encouragement, this tradition all their own had transformed my daughter completely, and healed her in obvious ways, including areas of confidence, academia and social development. I will always be grateful to Frank for the loving way he fathered my daughter. It is just one of the many reasons I cherish him as my St. Joseph. His golden years indeed had cast their sagacious warming hue on us all.

Our life together those *first* thirteen years was indeed our Eden, a truth revealed ironically and mysteriously during our *last* three years of living life backwards.

On that infamous day, what seemed as ordinary a day as any, we were taking my Jeep to be serviced. He was following me in his car. Both of us were stopped at a red light at the top of Indian Crest, only a mile or so from our home. Frank was hit from behind - and our life was forever changed. The thief came in the night, in a moment's flash, and a new journey began for us.

Frank's physical health seemed fine, but his personality and behavior began to change. His mental and cognitive capabilities had diminished, and we did not know what was happening. It was as if life was being jerked out from under us like a rug. I was frightened, confused, grieving the loss of my soul mate and protector. The possibility of Alzheimer's disease, or any mental disease, was just way beyond my capacity. My mother had suffered from depression her whole life, especially after Dad's death, and I had not handled it well. The thought of yet another case of role-reversal - becoming my husband's mother - terrified me; and I was sure I could not do *that*.

In retrospect, I can only imagine how frightened Frank must have been. How does it feel to be losing your mind, your very self? How does a strong, wise, leader and provider feel as the bloom is fading? How does one who has always been independent feel, becoming totally dependent?

Regretfully, at the time, I was unable to "go there" and was simply trying to survive the constant changes and mystery dealt by each new day.

During one of the most painful and traumatic periods of Frank's care, my Aunt Alice lost her son to a sudden heart attack. The next month, my older brother died of a sudden heart attack. Ten days later, my best friend and most dependable source of help with Frank, died suddenly of a brain aneurism. Like a zombie, I completed making my brother's arrangements in California, and then proceeded to my best friend's funeral; then, two weeks later we had my brother's funeral... Two months later, my prayer group leader died quickly of cancer. And just a few months after that, my sister Barbara's husband died of a sudden heart attack, and I spent a week with her in New York. It was like being under fire from a machine gun, with nowhere to hide. To keep the time perspective, this was five months before Frank died; he was bedridden and under constant home care. Barely afloat in my own grief of dementia, I was completely unable to absorb any more grief, much less to begin mourning the stacked up losses. Thankfully, I was also at that particular time caring for my 15-month old grandbaby who had started walking four months earlier... There was no rest for the weary, and no time for the bereaved.

Little Brantley Elizabeth provided the hope that got me up each day. One day when she was seven weeks old, I had captured an amazing photo of her, which was given to all the "dads" for Fathers' Day. In that tiny little

face were the most comforting little eyes bearing love, wisdom and hope –
and the loveliest tender smile that only a grandmother sees. I printed the
photo in many sizes, and put them everywhere. But the 8 X 10 framed
"canvas of joy" hung on the wall by my bed... Each morning, we would
look at each other; then I would laugh and say aloud, "You are so
precious!"

And Brantley and I would start a new day.

After months of medical exams and extensive neurological tests, and
comparisons to tests prior to the accident, doctors determined that because
of blows to the head Frank sustained in the car accident, the trauma had
triggered a rapid onset of severe vascular dementia. Inch by inch, I lost the
strong and wise man who loved and protected me, while being both
blessed and haunted by the false hope of lucid moments.

Lucid moments brought the greatest pain - to him, and to me. They were
the most important times to respond in compassionate love, and I clung to
every word as to life itself. Yet, it was the unpredictable and fleeting
nature of those moments which gave them haunt.

Pain brings self to the surface. My spiritual director, Father Angelus
Shaughnessy, taught me that there are three stages of pain: tolerating,
accepting, and embracing. Clearly, dementia is the slow death of the
person, though the physical body may be quite healthy. Yet, the person is
still alive, and could live for a very long time. These facts present realities
to the self that are frightening; and the natural response to fear is fight or

flight. My commitment to Frank and our marriage vows meant flight was not an option. I was committed, but what did that mean? For what seemed like a long while, the disease was managing us. We were tolerating it. Simply put, we were surviving. About the time I thought I knew how to manage a change in behavior, it changed again. It was like a long game of tennis at the net, and I was emotionally and physically exhausted. This is when I asked God to take over.

Part of my exhaustion was due to my own near death experience just months before the car accident. I had major surgery, and within a few weeks was hospitalized again with a mystery condition which I was told could kill me if I did not have a second surgery. It was not an option for me, physically; I had not healed from the first surgery and was told the second surgery would take longer. Family and friends had made great sacrifices to care for me and Frank. I told the doctor that it would be easier on my family if I died than if I had a second surgery, and I requested antibiotics instead. And I left it in God's hands. Well...I am still here, but it was a difficult year of the cross from start to finish.

I remember going into my foyer one day, and in front of my altar, with rolled up sleeves, looking up to Heaven and yelling, "Go ahead, keep sending me all this stuff! And I'm going to give it all right back to You because I CAN'T HANDLE IT!!"

It's funny now, but it wasn't then. I told God, "If Frank gets to where he doesn't know me, he'll have to go into a nursing home; or if he becomes incontinent. Or if he becomes combative." The Lord must have just smiled and said, "Okay." Thanks to the strong faith that God blessed me with, He was and is a real person in my life. When I was frustrated, I told Him. Once Father Angelus had told me that the commitment of love to care for my husband would develop in me heroic virtue. "It's what the saints are made of," he said.

I remember just "losing it" one particularly difficult day when I felt hopelessly exhausted. I cried out to God, "I am *no hero* - You've got the *wrong woman*!" When I told Father Angelus about this, he said, "You said that to the Lord? That's great that you can talk with Him." And Father Palmer, who ministered to Frank and to me as spiritual companion, encouraged me to express my grief and pain in my journal. It was through the support of these dear priests and others, and the support of my family and close friends, that I was able to accept God's will and embrace our cross of dementia. Clearly it was a call to love. And that call to love was offered to me first, as Frank's spouse, but also to every member of our family.

One thing is certain; I did not do it perfectly. But I was encouraged and comforted by Father Richard, who had once told me when I expressed feelings of inadequacy over being asked to lead a Lenten discussion group, not to worry about doing it perfectly or knowing all the answers. He said, "Ask the Holy Spirit to guide you, and then do the best you can with what you've got to work with." Those simple words of wisdom and hope apply to every task, and especially to the cross's call to love. I believe my greatest strength and ally, then as today, is my faith itself. Faith: simple, but sure.

As I gradually became more able through God's grace to accept and embrace our cross, I was able to share in Frank's passion and to enter into the present moment with *him*, wherever that was. I learned to see, hear, speak, and respond with my heart and not only with my brain. By choosing in love to share in his suffering and inviting him to share in my strengths, I was graced to love this man from the time of his greatest strengths and wisdom, backwards through his life. Clearly there were manifestations of the young man, the adolescent, the teen, the child, the toddler, the infant. Each required a unique level of care. My response was often very creative and was based on his need of the present moment. Dignity and respect for the man I loved and who loved me influenced all my choices. His safety, his health, his basic needs, his happiness, his soul - these were what mattered in each present moment.

It was providential that at the same time my husband went downhill, my first grandchild was born. As I cared for Brantley each day and watched her go forward in life, I witnessed the crossover of Alpha and Omega. Their needs were one and the same! God was present in each of them: The Creator seeking love from his creatures, from his sheep, from me.

In the springtime, I married Frank the man. And in the wintertime, I buried Frank the baby. And there also, present within, was the person of all seasons - Jesus, loving and needing to be loved by me. Forever I will thank God for slowing me down and helping me realize his gift.

Frank died at Christmas, and was honored with a holy and patriotic military funeral at our church. Later, surrounded by a beautiful white blanket of snow in the presence of those who loved him most, he was buried with full military honors at Arlington National Cemetery. After his death, he was awarded the Distinguished Service Medal for military service to Alabama. Also, the Andrew Jackson Council of the Boy Scouts of America in Jackson, Mississippi, honored Frank with the Golden Eagle award. He was also honored by BellSouth (now AT&T) and Senator Trent Lott for his unique contributions to Mississippi. Frank Edmonds the man: a story all its own.

This is our story. It is first of all a love story. Second, it is a gift of hope and encouragement offered to those who love and care for someone with dementia, as they live their own love story. May they each be blessed by God with abundant grace, strength, wisdom, and joy as He leads them in the light of their own cross.

CHAPTER
TWO
♥♥

MORNIN' GLORY

Catch 'em while you can
While they share their beauty
It's only for a moment
It's only if you're lookin'

How lovely is the bloom
Just after break of dawn
Brilliant blue and purple
Then in a moment – gone

Hearts with holes in green
They sing the whole day long
The mornin' glory song

©Ellen Marie Edmonds 2008

Chapter 2: **Signs of Change**

Quick - see the bloom! Savor its beauty in the present moment! Reflecting on the story of the lovely morning glory, I am reminded that no one on earth lasts forever. Gifted by the bloom, which flowers and fades, we cling to its everlasting fragrance.

The changes, they did come. As I share the following personal experiences, I must emphasize that the healthy Frank Edmonds was always seeking to help others. He was not responsible for his brain disease or its associated behavior changes. If he were reading along with us, he would also be laughing and learning with us. His outstanding record of contribution to society tells the story of his wisdom, strength, and competence. Yet, the sharing of his journey to littleness through dementia could be his greatest contribution, if it helps the thousands of others suffering as he suffered.

One of Frank's greatest gifts to me was his promise to take care of me for the rest of my life. Another was the wisdom he taught me simply through living life together. With him, I felt safe - for a precious little while. He was at peace with God, with himself, with his family, and with others. Little people and animals, perhaps all of nature, seemed drawn to his kind and gentle spirit. People frequently commented to me about how lovely we were together, how obvious it was that we cherished each other. He treated me as his queen, and he was surely my king. I remember thinking after just a few months of marriage just how lovely it was; and I knew that meant the excruciating pain of loss down the road. Because of our age difference, it seemed likely he would pass away first and I would be left widowed. But the idea of a head injury or dementia never occurred, thanks be to God. It would have terrified me. Ironically, the only real fear I ever remember Frank expressing was that of having a stroke and being a burden to loved ones. And he had one request: that he would never have to go into a nursing home. His own mother was in a nursing home when we were dating, so I asked, "Why was your mother in a nursing home?" And he replied that it had been the only option available. So I promised I would never put him in a nursing home unless it was the only option available. By the grace of God, I was able to keep that promise to him.

Life was indeed lovely on the mountain top of life. My faith in God as *Father* grew tremendously as I witnessed and received unconditional love from Frank. Strength, wisdom, security, kindness, affection, generosity, joyfulness, and commitment, just some of his character traits - he was everything to me that I imagined a loving father would be. This was important to my spiritual development, having been "put in charge" by my own father at 16, and then spending the rest of my life trying to learn how to "let go and let God." It seemed that the people I loved and depended on were always leaving me. Whether by choice or death, they were gone. My aunt told me that even at the young age of 2, my little brown eyes revealed a lack of trust. I was a very independent and strong child, which my father recognized when he left me his life duties. But there had come a time when, in one of my famous painful dialogues with God, I gave everyone back to Him so I wouldn't have to worry about when they were leaving. My then 16-year old daughter had totaled her car at 11 PM, after it flipped three times and landed in a ditch near Indian Crest – *that same infamous place where Frank's tragic accident would occur years later...* I remember staying up late, waiting for her to come home, and worrying why, what, where. Suddenly, at nearly midnight, the doorbell rang and there stood a strange man with my sobbing, debris-covered daughter. He had witnessed her auto accident, and had graciously stopped and retrieved my disoriented child from the ditch and brought her home. After a trip to the emergency room and assuring she was okay, I settled down a bit. It was the next morning that I had my "give it all back" chat with God. It really felt good, and to this day, I try to maintain a certain detachment with the people I love, recognizing that only God's love, presence, and trust are perfect and eternal. The love we share is God Himself; it is eternal. The physical presence and human capabilities are limited and temporal. It is the ultimate truth, I believe, which we are all called to learn in love. How we get there is God's design and His will.

With Frank, and with God's grace, I had learned to let go and to trust a human being in almost every way of life, even though it was only for a while. And then the mountaintop quaked a bit, and gave way to understanding the transcendence of God's infinite love to me through Frank. But first I had to trust. And in that trust, I had to commit to unconditional love with all its risks and sacrifice.

When memory loss surfaced, having had little or no experience in geriatric relations I assumed it was a normal age-related occurrence. An MRI by his neurologist confirmed this, but also revealed that a mild stroke had occurred some time earlier, which could accelerate memory loss. A medicine was prescribed to slow the process, and life proceeded.

About this time, I attended a workshop sponsored by the Mississippi Alzheimer's Association. There had still been no medical explanation for Frank's diminished cognitive skills, but I attended the workshop to prepare myself to respond to what I feared most. Frank was at that time on a prescribed drug to slow down memory loss associated with an earlier mild stroke. A conference speaker who was a physician had mentioned that when the patient is on a drug which works effectively for a period of time, and then diminishes, it is sometimes helpful to stop the drug for a couple of weeks, and then begin again with the lowest dose, building back to the highest. With Frank's sensitivity to drugs and his history of adverse reactions, this approach was approved by his physician and had proven to be a better option than switching to something new.

But on that ill-fated day on the mountaintop, we were stopped at a red light. Frank was hit from behind, and then hit my car, and I hit the car in front of me. Frank's seat broke, and the fall backwards jarred the back of his head. When he hit my car, the steel ashtray in his car dislodged from the drawer, striking his forehead near the frontal lobe and between the eyes. He was stunned and asked the driver why he had hit him, but otherwise seemed okay.

The next several weeks involved numerous doctors' appointments, dealing with assorted injuries, but with a particular focus on Frank's vision. What concerned his optometrist most was Frank's sudden inability to cooperate with her testing process, using procedures Frank was familiar with from previous exams. She asked at that time if "the General" had experienced a stroke or any significant health changes. After about 18 months of progressive cognitive loss and behavioral changes, his internist confirmed that the trauma to Frank's head had triggered a rapid onset of vascular dementia, and he was now in the advanced stages. The prognosis was that he would likely suffer a massive stroke at some point. Of course, by the time this information was received, our life had already changed 180 degrees. We had slipped way down the mountain...

Changes came on like a quake and its aftershocks. Truly, this was a frightening time of tolerating the pain and devastation in the darkness of uncertainty. What was happening? Why was it happening? What was next? How bad could it get? What was I supposed to do? I was always committed to doing the right thing for Frank, but what was that? What if I got hit by the infamous bread truck, who would care for Frank? As a Product Manager for many years, I had been well versed in worst case scenario planning. But what *was* worst case? It certainly seemed to be something far worse than death, and that was the worst I had ever considered. This was new territory for the cross of love. Later, as more facts were known, I was able to understand what could be ahead, then accept it mentally, and embrace it with my heart. The focus had to be on Frank, and I would share his pain.

As I describe the changes that occurred, I am reminded that this is all from *my* point of view. To Frank himself, it must have been terribly frightening, frustrating, and humiliating at times. Nevertheless, I can only describe my personal experiences.

There came a time when Frank began arguing with me about things that made no sense. One day, I asked him, "Honey, do you really not understand what I am talking about, or are you intentionally trying to agitate me?" He laughed and claimed the latter; in retrospect, I believe it was the first. People with vascular disease, including dementia, are often very bright and have excellent compensatory skills; they cover in ways transparent to the ordinary observer.

My husband loved afternoon naps. But there came a time that when he awoke, he thought it was morning and would take his daily medicines again. When I observed this once, he argued with me that it *was* the next day, and could not accept the proof of the calendar page. This was a serious yellow flag to me, because his health was at risk. And Frank had always managed his health with a scrutinizing attitude toward drugs. This was out of character for him.

Some other areas of concern were money and finance management. He was a brilliant executive of a major company, and managed his own affairs. But suddenly he was occasionally making decisions - or not making them - in areas that sent more warning flags. The interesting point with vascular dementia, however, is that there was always the presence of lucidity. It was totally unpredictable. Even six months before his death, when Frank's children came for their annual visit at Father's Day, he commented to me, "You know, they are good kids." He had not seen them for a year, but knew exactly who they were, even in his advanced state of dementia.

A "funny money experience" I recall is when a neighbor boy worked in our yard, meticulously shaping and trimming our landscape shrubs. I went to pay the young man, and he told me Mr. Frank had already paid him. I asked, "How much did he give you?" and he replied, "Three dollars." I was so embarrassed. "Oh, that was the tip," I said. Here's the rest," and I gave him $50.

An important point to make here is that there was a tendency for me to be embarrassed, ashamed, even humiliated by Frank's behavior. He was such a prominent citizen that many people knew his strengths. This downward spiral in mental capacity was shocking to everyone, and not easy to accept or respond to. It took a while, probably sometime into the "acceptance" period, before I realized that Frank's dementia was a disease of his brain, that God had allowed it, and it was not my fault. Of course, I did all I possibly could to preserve his dignity and respect, but in the end, this was part of Frank's life that I could not fix. My job was to love and care for Frank where he was, sometimes in a preventative way, but more often in a responsive way. This realization brought me tremendous relief.

Of all the signs of change that occurred, the one that most affected my heart and changed my vision of life, occurred in the kitchen. I was talking on the phone to an old girlfriend when Frank came running in and announced in a panic, "I can't find Ellen anywhere." My heart sank. At that moment, I became his full-time mother. Together we searched the house for Ellen. Back in our bedroom I asked, "Have you found Ellen yet?" He responded, still in a panic, "No!" Finally I just had to know. "Now, Frank - what is my name?" "You're Mack" he said. It was months later before I realized how preciously significant it was that when he could not find Ellen, he saw me as Mack - the friend who gave him hope and a place to live when Big Mama had died. As long as he knew me as someone who loved him, I was happy. About 15 minutes after the "lost Ellen" event, Frank said, "Hey, honey, let's go out to eat." Amazed, I asked, "Did you find Ellen?" He looked at me like I was crazy, laughed, and simply said, "Well, yes." I smiled - and then I swallowed. And then we went out to eat. Life would never be the same.

Bathing and dressing became a challenge early on. For some reason, Frank became ultra modest and insisted on showering in his socks and briefs. My initial response was pretty typical and drew resistance. But when I explained that his clothes would get all wet, he would submit. And it allowed him to save face. I learned that appealing to his emotions in a gentle and respectful way drew the desired response, when logic would not work. That became an effective tool for me, and preserved his dignity. This was particularly helpful in situations when quick action was necessary, or when I needed his cooperation in dressing, getting in or out of the car, etc. It is much the same with toddlers, who also do not like to be wet or dirty and often bow their backs when I try to put them in a car seat. Drawing them into the solution by appealing to their emotions is sometimes the only way to deal with a stubborn toddler!

There was sort of an obsessive compulsion to wear layers of clothing, which seems common to many folks with dementia. One day Frank was sitting in his recliner watching a golf match, fully clad and wearing a jacket, cap, and sunglasses. "Is the TV too bright?" I asked him. "No," he said.

"Why are you wearing sunglasses in the house?" I asked. And with perfect logic he responded, "Well, all those people are wearing them, so I am, too." And when I saw that they were also wearing jackets and caps, I had a new lesson of understanding. It was all a matter of meeting him where he was at any given present moment.

Our life had become a series of present moments. No memory, no past. No logic, no future; only the glorious now, with its fullness of joy and peace and certainty. I was learning the little way.

A most unusual occurrence was discovering Frank sitting in a chair in our bedroom, flipping repeatedly back and forth the pages in a book, frantically searching for something. After studying this behavior for a few moments, I observed that he was getting frustrated and anxious and flushed. I asked what he was looking for and he replied, "A place to put your clothes." So I calmly said, "Oh, look! You can put them right here in this drawer." He was fine and calmed down. But I had to wonder, where would that have ended in his brain? Could that sort of impossible thinking actually trigger high blood pressure and more vascular disturbance, if not an actual stroke or heart attack? At least, my intervention eased anxiety.

While my purpose of observing such behaviors was to see if I could help Frank get where he was trying to go, I hope the sharing of these observations is helpful to those in science and medicine who may be able to make meaningful and progressive associations between the observed actions and the activity of the patient's brain.

An interesting problem that surfaced involved the phone. Frank loved people and never met a stranger. If he answered a call, he might tell perfect strangers very private information. Because we had two lines, I began forwarding the first line to my cell phone when I had to leave the house, and would give him the phone with the second line. That way I could still receive all incoming calls, he could still call me, and I could still reach him on the second line. Prior to that, there were boxes of trash bags and light bulbs - you name it - being delivered to our house. Once I received a bill for $120 for trash bags he had allegedly ordered! I had heard it told, and I learned quickly first hand, that people prey on the elderly unless we protect them from themselves.

Another serious issue was Frank's getting lost in large stores, particularly Wal Mart. I would eventually find him outside, lost inside the store, or in a restroom - *which one* was always a mystery. Once I called my friend Lynn to come help me find him. And one time, he decided to go put his jacket in the car. However, it was not in *our* car. I always wished I could have been a fly on the wall when the jacket was discovered! We never recovered that jacket.

A couple of other discoveries I will share. Early on, Frank would ask me to repeat myself. It became more frequent, and finally I told him to get his hearing checked. He said it was my fault that I couldn't hear: I was short, he was tall, and I spoke too softly. Of course, that had not been a problem for the first 13 years of marriage, and I had not shrunk... His hearing was checked, and there was a removable blockage, which helped somewhat. But I learned after Frank's death, while attending a local dementia workshop, that the dementia brain receives communication in broken code, like a cell phone in a bad zone where the conversation sounds "chirpy." Because of receptor and nerve damage, they are able to receive some of the words the first time, some the second. And sometimes they fill in the gaps with their own words, which is why the dialogue is often difficult. Now, when an elderly person asks me to repeat or says they don't understand what I said, I am more understanding and will kindly and more slowly repeat myself. This could be me one day, and I hope people will treat me kindly. And after all, that's *Jesus* inside Who I am being kind to.

His appetite was quite healthy. About 20 minutes after a meal, Frank would ask me, "When are we going out to eat? I'm hungry." In the beginning I would "clarify truth" trying to reason with him, etc. As I grew in love and wisdom, or maybe just experience, I would give him fruit or crackers - a snack. That always seemed to please him. In fact, I do the same with my grandbabies, and tend to eat that way myself. Small, frequent meals can actually promote a healthier metabolism for everyone.

Activities like folding towels, handkerchiefs, etc. seemed to be good for Frank. He also liked putting things in drawers, which was helpful if properly channeled. These often repetitive activities stabilized his anxieties, and I suppose gave him a sense of accomplishment and purpose, as long as he did not get lost in an impossible cycle of frustration.

Recently, I was listening to a young woman whose father-in-law has Alzheimer's. She was describing the obsessive compulsion he had with straightening and aligning things on countertops. I asked what his work or hobbies had been, and she said he was a builder. It occurred to me he might enjoy working with magnetic building tiles, a favorite of both my grand daughters. It's something we can do together, or they can do alone – creative, colorful, and geometrically perfect, with magnetic edges that keep them together. They are simple and encouraging, because they stay together (until Riley decides to smash them.) So I recommended that they try them with the father-in-law, as something that could be both therapeutic and safe, while appealing to his innate bent and aptitude.

I remember, when checking out a day care facility, watching a sweet little lady who constantly swept the patio. It gave her purpose, and benefited those around her. As with toddlers, the best approach for the dementia adult was to provide a safe environment with suitable toys, stuffed animals or dolls, a broom for sweeping, towels to fold or anything else which kept them safely busy. When the kids are happy and content, I am too!

Isn't that what love is all about; bringing peace to another's life, and receiving it in return?

Finally, there was a phenomenon that occurred in the evening when Frank needed a nap. He would be in the middle of a sentence, and then finish with a totally unrelated point. I suppose his brain was tired. Ironically, my daughter and I used to *intentionally* do something similar when she was a teenager, just because it was funny and we understood that we made no sense. Her dad always took us so seriously, and his reactions were funny. But then came pay-back from the God of Second Chances… Ouch!

Anyone raising a toddler may recognize the above behaviors as being characteristic of the 2-4 years age group. For me, because I was caring for my little newborn grand daughter for the last 18 months of Frank's journey, I realized the parallels. In fact, as I was less and less able to care for Frank's physical care needs because of our size differences, I asked the Lord to honor my care for little Brantley as if I were caring for Frank: the same sacrifice, but in a package my size. I also asked the Lord to honor my care for *Frank* as if he were my father, since I had lost mine at 16. The Old Testament calls us to love and care for our father in his old age, when he loses his mind, with the promise that to do so is to atone for our own sins and the reward is eternal life. That is still my prayer today.

I would be remiss if I did not remember in gratitude how happy and loving my sweet Frank was, even to the end of his life. The behavior difficulties I experienced in the beginning were really due to a lack of understanding and change on my part. Once I realized that I could enter into his present moment – and that I was the one called to change and meet him where he was - it was smooth sailing…sort of.

CHAPTER
THREE
♥♥

MORNING SONG

The joyful doves greet me
The steady tune of the flute cord
Whooo - - whooooo - - - whoo!
You spread your wings
You dance! You bounce!
In, then out of the nesting place

Call to your lover - -
Will you come? Come!
The song is sung, the heart – necked
Or naked, if you choose
Revealed in the gift of your play

But your lover comes not –
Not in this moment
But in the heart that sings
Even in this moment

Ah, yes! You come in the hearts!
Then you fly to the distant tree
To the birthing place of the new song

Listen!

©Ellen Marie Edmonds 2008

Chapter 3: The New Reality

Morning had broken; it was a new day.

Living with an ever-changing daily life is the most exhaustive type of stress I have experienced. I found myself adapting more and more and more to the point of not really knowing who I was anymore. The only thing that was certain was change, and my faith. Consciously, I would not allow myself to enter fully into Frank's illness because I simply couldn't handle any more emotional pain or fear. But subconsciously, because I loved him so deeply, my heart walked with him in his darkest night, a walk that manifested itself in dreams filled with scenes of entrapment, panic, etc.

The early stages of his disease were very different from the later stages, and my response had to be equally different. But the first thing every morning, in the early days and in the bedridden days, I would embrace him and kiss him. It was there in that magic embrace that our eternal love remained unchanged; for the heart does not get dementia.

It had become clear to me in the early stage that I needed help caring for Frank. If I took him with me shopping, he often roamed or got lost. Like a very big toddler, he would run off. He was too big and strong for me to control, and I spent hours searching for him. Once at a shopping center he chose to stay in the car - but was gone when I returned. There were five stores to search before I found him!

At home, he required constant supervision as he began to take things apart, hide things, and turn things off or on. Once, I called an electrician out to fix my ceiling fan in the den with the cathedral ceiling. The kind young man said, "Ma'am, your fan was turned off at the unit. Someone must have pulled the chain." Could it have been my 6'4" hubby? That was a $75 lesson.

The new reality was that I had to make changes that would keep Frank safe, protect "things" from Frank, be able to manage our household affairs, and try to take care of myself. It was also during this time of change that my daughter was expecting my first grand child. Life would change again in about seven months when Brantley arrived.

Children can be a source of joy, hope, and happiness for everyone involved with dementia. But if the dementia patient becomes aggressive or combative as the disease progresses, I believe it is important to protect children from such episodes. I recall watching a PBS documentary on the subject of Alzheimer's disease in which the dementia patient was engaged in verbal combat with her 4-year old grandson. The narrator commented that the grandmother was herself behaving like she was 4 years old. Their exchange of painful "word bullets" resulted in the little boy bursting into tears and running away, and the grandmother not remembering what had happened. Such emotional encounters between a toddler and an adult whom he trusts and loves could cause serious psychological harm. Special efforts would be required to reassure the toddler that Grandma loves him, to let him know that Grandma is sick, and then to protect the child from future incidents.

Responding to new behaviors was as difficult as it was unpredictable. What had always worked for me in the past when faced with great challenges was to look around and see all the people who were successfully managing the same challenge. I knew that people all over the world were dealing with Alzheimer's and other forms of dementia, and most everyone seemed terrified and/or overwhelmed. Some resorted to nursing home care, and even that was difficult. That's all I knew about dementia. And that was enough to terrify me, as I began charting new waters.

Our dear friend Al worked with elderly and handicapped people for years, and his own mother was nearly 100. He and his wife Barbara were instrumental in suggesting possible solutions and giving me hope. And Al was very wise and compassionately clever. Once when Frank asked where the imaginary "lady in the back seat" had gone, Al observed me trying unsuccessfully to convince Frank there was no lady in the back seat. Al jumped in and said, "Frank, I think she had her own car and went home." Frank said, "Oh" and was quite content.

That was another great lesson I learned: keep it simple and make him happy. And that lesson was a free gift from sweet Al. God rest his soul.

Little by little, I accepted the reality that the man who loved and protected me was gone. I was now somewhat of a living widow with a big baby boy who himself was experiencing a sort of living death. This mental acceptance prepared me to change my expectations and convert my heart, so that I could love Frank in a new way, in a different way of marital intimacy.

Matters of intimacy and modesty, regardless of the relationship to the loved one with dementia, have to be looked at in a whole new way. From the simplest matter of maintaining proper hygiene to the more complex matter of sexual relations, everything is affected. No adult relishes the idea of having to bathe or be bathed by a parent or spouse. The reality of incontinence often sneaks in rather gradually, sending signals that diapers are on the horizon...and likely the resistance to them. And there will be many embarrassing and aggravating accidents, as with a toddler in training. Preparation and attitude adjustment are most important; however, due to pride and modesty issues with the loved one, the transition period may be difficult. There seems to be an increased level of modesty and combativeness associated with hygiene and incontinence issues, to the point that it sometimes takes a while to establish successful management. Still, hygiene must be maintained. As with potty training a toddler, creativity and distraction often help. It also helps to "save face" by saying something like, "Oh, no! Something spilled on your clothes and they are wet; let's change them." A friend once suggested to me that I keep a travel bag in the car, packed with things such as a change of clothes (head to toe!), cleaning supplies, and even a urinal to be prepared for the unexpected. What a great idea that was! In retrospect, those are almost the exact same things I pack in a diaper bag for my toddler grandbaby! Success starts with accepting the new reality and adjusting to it. And for a spouse, the reality of dementia in the marriage significantly affects the couple's sexual intimacy.

I remember reading a book about Alzheimer's disease, where the subject of sexual relations was being discussed. It was actually suggested that the couple seek help with a sex therapist! Now I may be missing something, but to me, based upon my own personal experience, that would be like taking a child or toddler to see Dr. Ruth... Such action, to me, would seem completely inappropriate - at the very least. It would be terrible to unknowingly inflict psychological and/or physical suffering upon a loved one who has become little and vulnerable. I suppose every situation could be different in this regard, and I am no expert on this subject. But in my opinion, based upon the new reality of who my husband had become - childlike and with diminished memory and reasoning capabilities - it was in *his* best interest that our love relationship transition to one of parent-to-child, rather than husband and wife. It is a complex issue, and one that should be discussed perhaps with a minister or spiritual companion, although I have found no one who feels competent to address the issue. My approach was to go with my heart in the present moment, based on the needs of my spouse and the stage of dementia. If intimacy resulted in what seemed to be expressions of confusion or shame, I would lovingly remind him of how grateful I was to God for bringing us together in marriage; and I would observe his response. If he still seemed confused or in any way anxious, that would clearly signal a call for compassionate relationship adjustment. There are many non-sexual ways to express your love for your beloved spouse. The first way is to consider their most important needs based on where they are in their disease, and to respond in a way that is physically and emotionally healthy for them. Some of the most famous collections of prose and poetry capture the beauty and loveliness of platonic romance. Again, I am no expert; but I have learned a lot about how to love these little people, and they are teaching me more every day.

CHAPTER
FOUR

♥♥

CHANT TO THE CHEROKEE

Here am I and there are you
Are you?
And were I there would you be there,
Or where?
Does your heart remember our glorious dance?
Shall we jitterbug today?
When our hands embrace, when our glances meet,
Are we dancing, Sweetie Pie?
In your nights that are longer than night itself,
Can you still find a flicker of my love?
Do you hear our song in your endless day,
Connecting the dots of our present moment?

My heart, my breath – they linger on...
In a world of memory and fantasy

Joy and sorrow
Roses and thorns
Trees

The doves sing for us, you know!
The melody of the Eternal Moment
Hugging us safely together... forever

I love you so much
And so long

©Ellen Marie Edmonds 2008

Chapter 4:   Embracing the Truth

That big tall Cherokee man; one moment here, then in a flash – somewhere else; yet always he would be found - in my heart...

When acceptance of our new way reached my heart, I knew that loving and caring for Frank would mean being his mother, and/or whoever else he might think I was in any present moment. But it also meant never losing sight of the man I loved, who loved me, and maintaining dignity and respect for "Frank the man" as he diminished into "Frank the baby." A new set of life values rose to the surface. Little by little, I let go of pleasures, things, and my very self. Life darkened a bit.

The truth was that dementia is a disease of the brain. My husband was dying. There was no cure. He would not get better. I was going to be a widow, and how awful those words were. My mother had been a widow; but I had only recognized that my father had died. Now I would understand that part of her life journey. "Widow" was one of those words that made me feel insecure, like the word "retired" did after 30 years of marriage to BellSouth.

Reflecting back today, I remember that when I finally did retire, I had to think of it as sort of a "death and resurrection" to a new life, like the caterpillar and the butterfly. In fact, I retired on Good Friday! But it was also April Fool's Day... And it was, indeed, the beginning of a different life.

As I prepared my heart for this new journey with Frank, I had no idea what the actual sacrifice could entail. Seeing, touching, and hearing the man who in the physical senses appears to be whole, is quite different from seeing, touching, and hearing with the heart. I remembered… and still longed for the man I could see. Our love would follow a new and simple path.

Research into Alzheimer's and other dementias revealed that there could be several *stages* of degeneration. If I had known *then* what I learned living through our journey, perhaps I could have planned and managed better, much as new or expectant parents would do. Clearly, caring for a baby requires great sacrifices of love, in several stages of development. We know this; we prepare ourselves as best we can; and still, we will experience the unexpected during the terrible twos, the teens, etc. Amazingly, Frank's dementia journey was almost the same process in *reverse*. And as with babies, where no two will crawl, walk, talk, etc. at the same time, Frank did not fit the *stage* categories. Having entered into Frank's journey with him, I observed *moments* more than *stages*. Reflecting in hindsight, his behavior moments could be categorized as typical of the mature adult, the adolescent, the teen, the child, the toddler, and the infant. As with children, the most difficult moments were those reflecting teen and toddler behaviors of rebellious independence and fearless confidence! That is when he most needed – and often resisted – supervision and protection. With the exception of the last 6-8 weeks of his life when the disease had ravished most of his brain, the behavior moments were varied among the categories and were unpredictable. With lucid breakthroughs, he could start over any time. On the positive side, loving Frank through this backwards journey in his life was a rare and fascinating adventure.

Bear in mind, all of this is written in hindsight with the hopes of helping others. At the time we were actually living the journey, I was simply keeping pace with his needs and responding as best I could. Essentially, I had to tune in and watch closely with all my senses, and meet him where he was. To me, that was just part of loving my husband "in sickness and in health."

Little phrases of praise delighted him. "I love you, Sweetie" was one of his favorites. He would always smile and say, "I love you, too." But once he surprised me with "I know you do. You love me more than anyone else in the whole world." That was profoundly inspiring and music to my soul - it made it all worthwhile; and I captured the moment in my journal. Visual stimuli, such as photos or stuffed animals, or laying the grandbaby next to him, would engage him. He particularly liked to wear patriotic shirts, and to see an American flag. Touching his hand or his face or hand worked well, too. And I would kiss him all day long, which he always responded to! I always told him my name, and asked him his – which he remembered until the end. "Norman Franklin Edmonds, Jr." he would say. I frequently told him how proud I was of him, how handsome he was, how I liked his shirt. I also bragged on his children and grandchildren, which he liked. Our communications had to be kept simple – short sentences, a few key words, things he could grasp and respond to. And I learned quickly not to ask "test questions" or to try to argue or prove points, etc. These areas of cognitive thinking were futile and simply caused conflict. Being right, etc., did not matter. His being happy, at peace, and well cared for did matter.

Embracing our new way of life was challenging, to say the least. Having to manage all of the business affairs that Frank had always handled, while caring for Frank and my new grandbaby, was a bit overwhelming. There were new financial challenges associated with his care. Outdoor household maintenance was often neglected, but I continued to have indoor cleaning help and yard care. I had to refocus on what was absolutely necessary with regard to time, energy, and money. Fortunately, Frank had established an excellent team of managers upon whom I could rely for continuity in critical areas. Our legal instruments were in order, which allowed me to make necessary decisions. And we had discussed many times issues regarding long-term sickness, death and medical decisions, and funeral matters. We had even discussed the possible horrors of cancer and senility, and openly discussed our desires. And we had discussed different scenarios regarding who might predecease whom, what actions to take, etc.

Many people involved with dementia have shared horror stories about legal, medical, financial, and even funeral matters which were not properly planned for. It is best to get such matters in order early on, and there are many elder law providers and geriatric physicians to assist in planning. Even prearranging funerals is beneficial, so that important decisions do not have to be made during a time of bereavement. Early in our marriage, we had equipped each other with the necessary tools for caring for the other if it became necessary. I was the "chosen one" for that eventual opportunity.

Once my heart had embraced the reality of our new life together, I began to see life from Frank's perspective. This was a huge step outside of my self, and it had to happen in its own time, in God's own time. In essence, I dared to let my heart walk in Frank's shoes for the duration - whatever that meant. It would be difficult, but we would do it together, all three of us: Frank, me, and the Holy Spirit, in the Trinitarian love of marriage.

Probably one of the greatest spurts in my personal spiritual walk came at this time of embracing the truth that my husband, whom even I admired and depended upon so much, could no longer guide and protect me with his great wisdom. There were many regrets for not having asked him more questions and recorded more family stories; but that was now spilled milk. Together, we would live our new life in the little way, in every little moment we had left together. And having embraced this truth of our tiny new world, I realized we would be loving each other more intimately than ever – united with our souls, in the little way of eternal Love.

CHAPTER
FIVE
♥♥

GOLDEN HEARTS

For all the times, the ways
I have hurt you
Will you please forgive me?
"Yes" nodded, so surely
So lovingly – so Fatherly…
I forgive you, too
Though nothing I recall

Thank you, Sweetie
I love you so much
I know you do –
You love me more
Than anyone else in the world

Spoken words
So clearly, so lovingly – healing…

♥♥

The hands clasp the seal
Of the souls' wisdom
The hearts beat out
The gift of love we share

In the day's youth
The sun pours out its light
Shining, warming,
Caressing the living blooms
Which in the night time fading
Find their hope
In the moonlight dance

©Ellen Marie Edmonds 2008

Chapter 5: Faith, Hope, and Forgiveness

Hoping in the moonlight dance…seeing that flicker of love in the darkness of pain; forgiving… living… in faith…faith in God, faith in Frank, faith in myself. The Trinitarian faith we shared together fueled me with hope, one night at a time.

One's faith in God is a very personal matter, and that relationship with Him is unique to each of His creatures. As stated in the Vatican II document, *Declaration on Religious Freedom*, "The human person has a right to religious freedom. This right has its foundation in the very dignity of the human person, as this dignity is known through the revealed Word of God and human reason." It is God Himself who calls each one *to* Himself, and the rest is in our free-will response. God has given me a bouquet of family and friends to love and be loved by, all with different faith and cultural backgrounds. Having roots from Jewish, Catholic, Greek Orthodox, and Episcopalian ancestors (and some gray roots, too…); and having relatives of other faiths, I have great respect for and learn from others who faithfully live out their relationship with God. Our dialogues are open and respectful, and key to our friendships. In our quest for truth, we learn from each other; for although the *church* has all of truth, no one *person* has all of truth. Wisdom and truth, I believe, are revealed most beautifully in the interdependencies of sacrificial love; love depending on love, which is God Himself.

Pope John Paul II wrote and spoke prolifically about matters of faith and love. He cautioned his flock not to argue over differences among the many

Christian denominations and churches; rather, let us all focus on our *baptism in Christ*. Loving others whose faith is very *different* from mine is often sacrificial in and of itself; likewise, loving me must be equally sacrificial for them.   But the fruits can be plentiful. For the last several years prior to retiring, I was allowed under the Telephone Pioneers organization to start a "lunchtime inter-faith devotional" for employees. It was a thirty-minute meeting with a speaker, prayer, and fellowship, with a diverse group of faith backgrounds. For our first meeting, a Franciscan friar delivered the devotional, and gave blessed rosaries to everyone. He told them that if they did not know the Rosary Prayer, to simply say "Jesus I love you" on every bead; and then he said "maybe Ellen will teach you about the rosary some time." Sure enough, at a later meeting, the speaker cancelled; so I gave a devotional about the Rosary Prayer – the role God gave Mary in salvation history, how the prayer started, how the mysteries contemplate the life of Christ through the eyes and heart of His mother. The response was favorable and apparently clarified a lot of misconceptions. It was a delight on a weekly basis to share our faith and to pray together, with respect for each other's faith walk.   Once when no speaker was available, I opened the meeting simply for intercessory prayer. Each one presented a petition, and then each began to offer vocal prayer. That image of so many hearts beautifully connected to Heaven in prayer continues to bless me.   Truly, there is One spirit, but many gifts…

Our community is blessed to have many pilgrimage and retreat sites, frequented by people from all over the world – including me!   As somewhat of a "hummingbird" I know where to find the "nectar." Interested in meeting other "brothers and sisters" I often go to the monastery and introduce myself to strangers; and a new friendship in faith begins. The faith journeys of others fascinate me. Many, many longtime friendships began just that way. I am very grateful for those friendships, as well as all those who have helped shape and nurture my faith before and during the painful cross of dementia.

During a retreat I attended hosted by the Sister Servants of the Eternal Word at Casa Maria in Irondale, Alabama on the subject of "Suffering," the retreat master explained how *suffering* is only possible because we have *loved*, and that *God is love*. Therefore, God is present in our suffering. When we embrace suffering as the carrying of our own cross, we can unite our suffering with that of Jesus Christ on the cross, and share in the redemptive aspect of suffering. Knowing this, gave new purpose to my own cross, and lightened the load I was carrying.

As a Christian, I know the call of Jesus to serve *Him* by serving the sick, the lonely, the poor, and the imprisoned. Matthew 25: 34-40, tells us: "...for I was hungry ...I was thirsty...I was a stranger... I was naked... I was sick...I was in prison... Truly, I tell you, just as you did it to one of the least of these who are members of my family, you did it to me." Knowing it and *living* it are not equal. *Seeking* Him, we will *find* Him; then we can *serve Him.* To serve Christ in my *husband*, I had to seek Christ in my *husband*.

I remember first realizing the biblical truth that King Jesus came, not to be served, but to *serve.* Following *Christ* meant being a *servant.* Serving Him meant serving the "least" among us in society. True, that means the sick, the hungry, the poor, the lonely, and the imprisoned; applied to my life and God's call to me; it means my spouse; my parent; my child. It's my brother; my sister; it's my neighbor. Simply put, the least among us is the hurting human being right in front of me, whom I am called to love. And how do we love? We *serve*. Serving equals sacrificing equals loving.

Over the years when Father Angelus was at EWTN, his sermons frequently taught the principle that only a humble, grateful heart can truly love. I can recall having passionately declared my desire to truly know, love, and serve Christ with my whole life; I had no idea what that meant. Today, I know we must *become little* before we can know the *little way* of humble, grateful Love. Years later, while facing the challenge of my husband's dementia, I was reflecting upon that earlier conviction to serve; and I was reminded of a related significant event. Following a Mass which Father Paul had offered for babies in heaven, each of us present had been "recommended in prayer" for our own particular petition. My request had been "for the heart of a humble servant..." Wooooah! Lesson learned there in hindsight: be careful what we ask for – we will be given the gift ... *and* the work to go with it! Most significantly, we will also be equipped in *grace* to do that work, to embrace and carry our cross.

Embracing our cross of dementia as a call to *love* meant a call to love *God*. That knowledge was significant to me. It meant that He was always there with us, and that He would guide me in the simplest, the surest way of love. I had to prepare in love to suffer, and let *faith* replace *fear*. With love and faith came the light of hope to endure the darkness. That hope, that trust, gave me tremendous courage to continue on, knowing I was not in the driver's seat, but merely a vessel in God's hand, asked to do His will.

I did not always do it well, but I did the best I could with what I had to work with: my humanity, my limits, my pain - and faith. And the peace came from believing that even my poorest efforts were accepted by God, and were within His permitted will for me and for Frank. And the faith of others, who I knew were praying for us, strengthened me; I was not alone.

Life and my schedule eventually became so convoluted that my prayer life was affected, and I was not able to attend Mass everyday, as I once had. So, I chose to offer my care of Frank and of my grand daughter, my struggles with managing the rest of my life all alone - as my prayer. It was all I could give; it was all there was. Sometimes, just breathing was prayer.

Ever since I was a little girl I have prayed the *Guardian Angel* prayer. I believe in the powerful role of the angels, especially the role of our personal angel. Once, at the suggestion of Mother Angelica, I asked my guardian angel to reveal his name to me; he is Daniel. In those days when I felt most fragile, I called on him *by name* to help and carry me:

> *Daniel* - Angel of God
> My guardian dear
> To whom God's love commits me here
> Ever this day be at my side
> To light and guard
> To rule and guide – Amen

Even today, in caring for little Riley, any time I ascend or descend the stairs carrying her, I send up a plea of "Daniel, please help me." In fact Riley is so strong - and strong-willed – that sometimes I also ask *her* guardian angel for help! Prayer in faith is powerful. For years, Frank and I had prayed together a morning prayer of thanksgiving to God, consecrating ourselves and all our children, grandchildren, great grandchildren, and godchildren - born and unborn - to God through the Two Hearts, Jesus and Mary. We prayed for all of us to be filled with the Holy Spirit, that we may all know, love and serve God and do His will for us. It was a powerful faith booster, placing all our loved ones and our very selves, in God's will.

When the crisis of dementia came on the scene, it was a consolation to be able to frame the experience within the context of my faith in God's will. Clearly, this experience was either *ordained* by God or *permitted* by God for us, so that we may draw closer to Him in love. And love, like truth, is often painful. In those lowest, most painful moments, Love is listening. And I *knew* He heard my simplest prayer: "Thy will be done, Lord."

Only the birth of my daughter, of receiving the gift and the cross of motherhood, compares to the life lessons of this dementia journey. Perhaps the reason is that, as Mary loved Jesus, a mother loves her child more than anyone else does. Embracing Frank's dementia - accepting it in my heart and acting in love - let me love him as a mother, as Mary loved Jesus, as Ellen loving Jesus in Frank.

These truths give profound meaning to my life. As Saint Paul tells us (1 Corinthians 13: 13), there is faith, there is hope, there is love; and the greatest of these is love. I believe the *capacity* to love – one's ability to endure a commitment of sacrifice and suffering - is commensurate with one's faith in God and acceptance that *everything* is in accordance with His will, ordained or permitted. And the hope which comes from knowing He is always in control has divine meaning and purpose. Human instinct might send warning flags of "suffering ahead" and tell us to run from the situation. If the relationship has been difficult and painful, the natural response might include an attitude of vengeance. "He hurt me; now let him hurt." Or, "she was not there for me; now it's her turn to feel abandoned." Recognizing that these are normal human responses to pain and suffering, it is important to try to see the situation in the context of faith and hope, calling on God to help us do the right thing. And it almost always begins with *forgiveness*.

It amazes me how little society talks about the need to forgive others. The focus seems to always be on obtaining forgiveness. We want to be forgiven – by God, by those we love, by our very self. Yet, when we look at what Jesus says about the matter, the emphasis seems to be on first forgiving. In teaching us the Lord's Prayer, Jesus tells us to ask the Father to "forgive us our trespasses, as we forgive those who trespass against us". And in Matthew 6:15, Jesus explicitly says, "If you forgive others their transgressions, your heavenly Father will forgive you. *But if you do not forgive others, neither will your Father forgive your transgressions.*"

Now, *that* is a contingency to ponder…

I am reminded of Father Angelus' teaching about love, which is discussed in Chapter 6. Love is a gift, the willingness to *give*. Of the seven kinds of giving: forgiving, giving in, giving up, giving away, almsgiving, thanksgiving, and life giving: the most *necessary* form of giving – as told to us by Jesus Christ himself – is *forgiving*. It is a condition of our *being forgiven* by God.

Clearly, we are called first to forgive. Then God forgives us. It is true also that we are called to confess and repent of our own sin, to express our sorrow to those we have hurt, to change our heart and repent. But whether or not another human being forgives me is a "soul matter" between that person and God. My business is to forgive, which means I may even have to forgive someone who has not accepted my apology and who has not forgiven me. Forgive; and we shall be forgiven by God.

Blessed Mother Teresa, in her ministry to the poor dying in the streets of Calcutta, zeroed in on this fundamental requirement to forgive in order to attain eternal life with God. I remember her sharing about having ministered to a dying man, and asking him if he wanted to spend eternity with God. He had said "yes." Mother had told the dying man he must forgive everyone who had ever hurt him. When the man said he could never forgive his son who had hurt him terribly, Mother Teresa told the man he *had* to forgive his son, so that God would forgive *him* of his *own* sins. And so, the man had come to realize on his deathbed, through the active love of Mother Teresa, that it is in forgiving we are forgiven.

This example of Mother Teresa's work of mercy with the dying stuck in my heart. Once when I was going to visit a dear friend who was dying, and who had been un-churched for years, I had no clue of what I would say. I stopped in the chapel and praying before the Blessed Sacrament, asked God what I should say to my friend. Suddenly the Holy Spirit recalled to me the story Mother Teresa had shared about the dying street man. On my drive to Atlanta, I prayed that my friend's heart would be ready, and I asked the Holy Spirit to guide us in our visit together. When I asked my friend the question, "Do you want to spend eternity with God?" he responded, "Yes, but I'm afraid it's too late. I've blown it." I responded, "You're still alive, aren't you? It's not too late. You simply have to forgive everyone who has hurt you, and ask God to forgive you." Oddly, like the man in Calcutta, he named one person whom he just could not forgive. Remembering Mother Teresa, I said, "But you *have* to forgive him. Even God will forgive him if he asks him to. You have to forgive him so God will forgive *you*." Then I asked the questions again. This time, he responded with a resounding and passionate "Yes!" as he squeezed my hand with hope. Then I gave him a crucifix and medal from Medjugorje, blessed by Pope John Paul II while I was in Rome, a holy card with the "Prayer Before a Crucifix", and a bottle of holy water. The holy card depicted Calvary, and my friend inquired about the people at the foot of the cross. In my sharing with him about that greatest moment of God's sacrificial Love, and how his Mother Mary, the apostle John, and Mary Magdalene stayed with Jesus to the end of his suffering, my friend got the "crash course" in Christian love and forgiveness. Later, at his funeral, the presiding minister told me he had visited my friend often in the last few weeks of his life; and he said that at every visit, my friend would show him the holy cards and the sacramentals, and tell the story. The minister said my friend had died wrapped in faith, hope, and love. And I gave glory to God, and thanksgiving to Mother Teresa for her witness; may her gift continue through all who read and respond to this testimony of forgiving.

As Frank's spiritual companion, I had recalled this need to forgive. We had a specific moment of general forgiveness to one another, which I recorded in my journal. Over the years of our married life, we had quite humbly discussed the pains we had given and received, in relationships with our family and friends and others. When two people get together, pain eventually happens. Pride rises; both want to be right, etc. It's just that simple. The longer one lives, and the more people one knows, the more opportunity there is for love and forgiveness. In the evening of Frank's life, he had come to realize and share with me so many profound truths about these matters. Many times, he had been hurt by direct behaviors or known actions of those he loved; and he simply chose to accept the weaknesses, the mistakes, and love them for their goodness. He often called them "growing pains" and said that sooner or later, we all experience and learn from such mistakes. The soul journey is the same for each one of us – reaching that point of humble self-reflection before God, forgiving our self and forgiving others, and asking God to forgive us as we gratefully accept his mercy.

In Frank's acceptance of his own lonely cross, of being physically separated from loved ones around the country and mentally separated from his own body– he taught me so much about the peace which comes from faith and hope. He showed me how to find joy in each new moment of life and love that we shared with God; grateful for the beauty present, while remembering in faith the beauty of life past, and hoping in the beauty of life eternal.

Father God, help us to forgive – that we may be strengthened in faith and hope to answer your call to serve in love.

CHAPTER
SIX
♥♥

B-r-o-k-e-n

Your brokenness
Is the soil for my Seed
My Love sprouts and thrives
In your dark night
Your tears give water
And form buds on My Vine
Your sorrow is the ladder of thorns
On the path to redemption
Your heart is the chalice
That receives My Love
Your love gives the Light
Where buds bloom in darkness
In your brokenness
You are Me
In your brokenness
You are Love
In your brokenness
I AM yours
Broken,
We are One Love

©Ellen Marie Edmonds 2008

Chapter 6: **Spiritual Direction**

Broken. Exhausted. How does one cope without faith in God? In those moments of total brokenness and exhaustion, I would often visit the adoration chapel – sometimes at 3 a.m. – just to cry out to the Lord. With my buddy the journal, I would listen and write. Sometimes, too tired to make the visit, I would make a "spiritual visit" from my bedroom. As I later learned through my writings, He was always there with me. And I would be refreshed.

Thanks to my already strong faith and having received sound spiritual direction, this journey became a faith-walk matter, a commitment to serve God through my love for Frank. Truly, my relationship with Christ Himself was my greatest source of spiritual direction, followed by my relationship with His mother Mary. But many priests, religious, and saints have also influenced me spiritually. In fact, when all seems lost, I find particular hope in Saint Paul – who was once the great sinner Saul; Mary Magdalene – whose sins were forgiven because of her great love; and King David – a man after God's own heart, whose sins of adultery and murder were forgiven. They give hope to all of sinful humanity, especially in times of trial and the stress of life.

In my situation of enormous stress due to my husband's illness, it was critical that I maintain relationships with family and friends who would listen and encourage me, and exercise my brain and vocabulary (since neither Frank nor my grand baby talked much). It was equally important to have a spiritual compass, a sounding board, and a sage who would direct and encourage me in my faith. That person for me during our dementia journey was Father Angelus Shaughnessy, O.F.M. Cap., who was at the time Father Guardian at the Annunciation Friary and EWTN television network.

Time after time, I found myself in the chapel of Our Lady of the Angels monastery praying before the crucifix and asking "Jesus crucified, give me your patience." Father Angelus kept me on track and encouraged me to keep going. He is a walking treasure of faith and a blessing to the church, and to me personally.

Two points which stand out among many discussions we had, often with a squirming baby Brantley in my lap, are as follows:

(1) Devoting myself to caring for Frank and my grandbaby was the sacrificial love that developed "heroic virtue" in the saints and,

(2) I must share with others what I have learned through contemplating God's presence in my journey, and as revealed in my journal writings.

I knew about lots of different saints. But, *heroic virtue* – what was *that*? In researching the term, I found "virtue" defined in paragraph 1803 of the Catholic Catechism, as a "habitual and firm disposition to do the good." There are three *theological* virtues – faith, hope, and love/charity, which are given directly to us by the grace of God; and there are four *cardinal* virtues –prudence, justice, fortitude, and temperance, which are moral virtues acquired by human effort through the exercise of our intellect and will. With regard to the term "heroic," one definition I found in an old World

Book Dictionary was: "unusually daring or bold; using extreme means to get a necessary result." In my words: "courageously driven by love."

It was interesting to note that all *moral* virtues lead back to the cardinal virtues; and *all virtues* – lead back to the theological virtue of *love*. Isn't this what Saint Paul is saying in 1 Corinthians 13: 13 "There are in the end three things that last: faith, hope, and love; and the greatest of these is love."

It was also interesting to note that each of the seven virtues has an opposite bad habit, which is called a *vice*. To correct a *vice*, one must practice its opposite *virtue*. Remembering that all virtue is rooted in the God-given virtue of *love*, it's fair to say that practicing love by exercising the seven ways of giving will certainly develop virtue and conquer vice! Father Angelus once gave me the following "Giving/Loving" guidelines to help me see this principle in action, not just in our dementia journey, but in all of life:

1. Most *Necessary* Giving:	**Forgiving**	
Associated vice:	**Anger**	(Aggressive Instinct)
2. Most *Difficult* Giving:	**Giving In**	
Associated vice:	**Pride**	(Power Instinct)
3. Most *Proving* Giving:	**Giving Up**	
Associated Vice:	**Sloth**	(Escaping Instinct)
4. Most *Clever* Giving:	**Giving Away**	
Associated Vice:	**Greed**	(Possessive Instinct)
5. Most *Practical* Giving:	**Almsgiving**	
Associated Vice:	**Gluttony**	(Survival Instinct-eating, drinking)
6. The *Best* Giving:	**Thanksgiving**	
Associated Vice:	**Envy**	(Territorial Instinct)
7. The *Greatest* Giving:	**Life-Giving**	
Associated Vice:	**Lust**	(Sexual Instinct)

The one I seem to have to practice the most often is forgiving. Being a very sensitive person, it is easy to be hurt; pain turns to anger, which can result in aggressive behavior. When I'm feeling angry and acting aggressively, I have to stop and ask myself, "why am I angry, why am I hurting, who do I need to forgive?" and then do it. That exercise brings amazing healing.

All that research about virtue came right back to this thing called love: saints are made of heroic virtue because they *love* heroically. It is noteworthy here to quote one of Mother Angelica's classic teachings: "We are *all* called to be saints; *don't* miss the opportunity." I was called to love Frank heroically, that is, daringly and boldly, and with extreme means if that is what was necessary to love him. Whew! Some might say we were daring, bold, extreme... but in the end, I simply did the best I could, guided by faith, hope, and love. And I left the rest to Management. It is all any of us can do.

So, here we are, Father Angelus, sharing this journey with others. I am forever grateful for your fiat to God!

Several other priests have provided different forms of spiritual direction, including Father Palmer, who ministered to Frank and me in our parish, anointed Frank several times, and was there at his death, his funeral, and his burial at Arlington National Cemetery. The common thread of all Father Palmer's messages is the reminder that "God is Love." It was Father Palmer who encouraged me to journal for its spiritual and therapeutic benefits. He has blessed me, and my family, with the great gift of spiritual companionship during this journey; we are forever grateful.

Father Angelus once told me that my greatest strength is my faith. I am grateful to the many holy people – living and deceased – who have loved me, taught me and prayed for me. By God's grace, I believe and I hope, one moment at a time. My godparents, Luke and Marian Peavey, were also instrumental in the early development of my relationship with Jesus and Mary. Over the years of many job transfers with the telephone company, I was blessed by the gift of priests, brothers, nuns and sisters, and holy friends who taught me and loved me in faith.

It was Father Richard who graced me with the *understanding* of the presence of the Holy Spirit within me, which changed my faith and life forever. The Gospels came alive; Christ became real, in a way I could follow, knowing His spirit was in and with me, always.

Father White's profound wisdom in every homily I have been blessed to hear continues to nurture me. It was he who told me in my 30's that what kind of work we do in life is not what is most important; what matters most is that we do it in love. That life lesson and his teaching about the Christian cross – where our vertical relationship with God intersects our horizontal relationship with others – continue to provide a framework of hope and direction for living this life of faith.

Father Paul, whom I met in the Holy Land just prior to his entering seminary, shared with us his journey of formation, and we shared with him our support as his extended family. It was through him that I learned another foundational teaching: God doesn't always answer your prayer with what you want, any more than your earthly father would give you everything you want. I had gotten pretty frustrated with the "ask, seek, knock and you *shall* receive" at the time… Later, God would show me that the "shall" is connected to the "seek, knock" which are the actions, the sacrifice required of love. Pray and wait and accept; that is the formula.

And then there is the quiet, faithful Father Michael, offering frequent Holy Masses for Frank, before and after his death, and also for me. God bless him for his perseverance and his steadfast agape love.

Many, many wonderful holy priests have taught me well. Complementing their gift of priestly spiritual direction has been my love for and from Jesus' mother Mary, who He Himself gave to us while hanging from the cross. I believe that every word Jesus spoke *from the cross* is particularly critical to living the Christian life, including the giving of His mother to us through the apostle John.

I want to clarify that we *do not* worship Mary or consider her to be some goddess or our savior. Rather, recognizing the very significant role she was chosen by God to play in salvation history, we honor Mary with love and respect as God first honored her when he chose her to be mother of His only Son. And I don't want to be at the Pearly Gates having to answer the question, "So, tell Me, Ellen – exactly what is it that you don't *like* about My mother?"

Mary has modeled for me not only motherly love in general, but love for her son, Jesus. No other earthly creature ever loved Jesus more than His mother Mary. And no other human was chosen by God to participate in

His plan for salvation the way Mary was chosen. And no other human responded to God's call to love the way Mary has. Ponder the fact that, when God became man - that moment of the Incarnation, which took place first in Mary's heart with her "yes" and then in her womb - there was no one present except Mary, the angel Gabriel, and God. *Who do we suppose told the world what had happened?* Mary was the only human witness to this cornerstone dogma for the entire Christian faith. To take it a step further, I am grateful that Mary was not only willing to respond to God's enormous call to love, but also that she was willing to share with the rest of us humans the truths of what had happened. To me, she is the awesome model of perfect humility. I want to know, love, and serve God in the motherly way of His beloved and chosen servant Mary.

I came to know Mary as my heavenly mother in Mexico City on a pilgrimage to the shrine of Our Lady of Guadalupe. It was Monday, June 9th, the birthday of my deceased earthly mother Helen. The tour bus was on the way to the shrine for the first time. I was not particularly interested in the tour guide's discussion of Aztec architecture and I was missing my mother deeply that day. So I began praying the Joyful Mysteries of the Rosary Prayer for my mother. Suddenly in the second decade, very clearly in my heart came the words, "I am your mother, and you are coming to see me." There was this "dialogue of hearts" for a few moments, which graced me with the knowing that on earth, Helen and Ellen were mother and daughter. But in eternity, we are sisters - and Mary is our Heavenly mother. I burst into tears, which I had to explain later to my friend in the seat next to me. "It's okay – I'll explain later," I had said. This joyful experience – a joyful mystery all its own – became known for me as my

"Moms' Birthday," for it was the day my earthly mother was born on earth and the day my heavenly mother was born in my heart. It was another Alpha Omega truth.

I believe that for those of us who have lost our earthly mothers, Mary's heart waits to embrace us as outstretched arms. And we are never too old to need a hug from Mama.

Pope John Paul II "the great", who entrusted his papacy to Mary's heart in his motto *Totus Tuus*, calls this way to Christ the "School of Mary." In reading his Apostolic Letter, *Rosarium Virginis Mariae*, one can truly learn to contemplate the life of Christ – the holy Gospels – through the eyes, the heart, and the love of Mary for Jesus. If I can respond to the call of Love, in the motherly way of Mary, it will surely require first loving God the Father through Jesus her Son. In Holy Scripture we are fed by His Word. In Holy Communion, or the Eucharist, we are nourished by His body. In the Rosary Prayer, we contemplate all of His life through the joyful, luminous, sorrowful, and glorious mysteries. Fully equipped, we go forth doing the best we can. And when we fall, we humbly get up and start over... It is the *way* sinners become saints.

Jesus Christ, son of God, have mercy on us! Mother Mary, pray for us!

CHAPTER
SEVEN
♥♥

♥♥♥ Heart Tracks ♥♥♥

If i look
With my eyes
But see
With my heart;
If i listen
With my ears
But hear
With my heart;
If i talk
With my mouth
But speak
With my heart;
And, if still
i know not their pain
All was done in vain…

If i step in their shoes,
Walk a while with my heart –
Then…
None will be in vain
For all will be in Love

Oh, Heart!
Whose shoes shall we wear today?

©Ellen Marie Edmonds 2008

Chapter 7: **The Call to Love**

This thing called "love." What does it *really* mean? For me, it means a commitment to give myself to another, to do what is needed for the one I love, to make sacrifices. *How* to love is another matter.

The journey of faith has many branches. At this time in my life, the most important quest is to get it right about this thing called "love." It's a word used in a variety of ways to describe "what" it is. Rarely is there much said about "how" to do it and "why" it matters. There is nothing I can add to what has been revealed to us about what love is or why it matters. What I had to learn through this journey was *how* to love, how to get it right. It is a quest and a journey that continues until death.

As a person always seeking the practical application in learning, my soul remains restless over this matter, because every person in my life calls for a new "how." The situation, the call to love, is *my* cross. How I respond to the call is the *carrying* of *my* cross. And it's always right in front of me. The most difficult crosses are often associated with those we love most, our family and closest friends.

There are excellent writings about love. First and foremost is the Holy Scriptures. The Old Testament God is commanding us to love through the law of the Ten Commandments; the New Testament God is loving us by becoming one of us in the person of Jesus; many teachings of Jesus and of Saint Paul, are commanding us to love as God loves us, and are describing some of what love is - and is not - in the book of 1 Corinthians. Jesus teaches about love in Matthew 25 through "sheep and goats" who did or did not see and love Him in the poor, the sick, the lonely, etc. And Jesus demonstrated the ultimate call to love *us* in the giving of His very self to death on a cross, so that we might have eternal life.

For me, this "call to love" primarily comes directly from my creator, not just as a command to obey but also as a desire to please Him. In some ways, simply complying with the commandment takes away the gift. I *choose* to love, with my free will, in order to please God. But beyond that, perhaps in a more human way, I am called to love in response to those who love and have loved me. In Frank's sickness, I was also called to love him in response to how unconditionally he had loved me.

Frank had loved me as no other person ever had. He was my Saint Joseph, on whose feast day we had in fact married. It was through Frank, living life with him, that I realized God's love for me. This man, though retired, would rise in the morning and get fully dressed, simply to prepare my breakfast and spend time with me before I went to work. He would walk me to my car every morning, and wave to me as I left. That image stayed in my heart all day and drew me home at night. Finding ways to please me gave him joy. Not a holiday passed without a "happy" appearing somewhere. I never figured out where he hid those floral baskets that would be waiting for me in the morning, in the kitchen or bathroom. And hiding a new bottle of perfume under my pillow – just because he noticed the other one was empty – thrilled me! The man spoiled me, but in a healthy way. He never, ever expressed a need or desire to get a break from me, or get away by himself. We gave respite to each other, and we prayed to our God together. The care he had for me, that we had for each other, ran deeply and carried with it total dedication and commitment. In the 16 years we were married, I can recall only one day that we did not talk to each other by phone: I was in Italy - and none of the airport phones would work! Whether I was in Israel or Bosnia, or anywhere in the world, we talked every day. A priest had once told me that when you go on vacation, you don't take a vacation from God. God is love; and we never took a vacation from our love for each other. I could write an entire book on the goodness of Frank Edmonds. Frank loved me in a way that compelled my heart to love back; I couldn't help myself. The call to love him - to sacrifice for him - was in itself a pleasure, a gift to my self.

But was I called to "die" that my husband might have "life?" This question I ponder even today with each new call to love, with each new cross. For, as the wise Father White once taught in a homily, the real cross we bear as Christians is where our vertical relationship with God intersects our horizontal relationship with others. There, in that cross point, is where two hearts meet. It is where the love of-and-for God meets the love of-and-for man. If the energy of that cross point, that present moment, could be bottled, the world would need no pills, no food, no gas or oil. For in the heart resides Omnipotent Love, Who is God Almighty Himself. We must only realize Its presence and Its call and respond to It with our fiat, as Mary herself did when God became man - first in her heart, then in her womb. It first takes place in the heart, where God's call is embraced.

Several years ago, I realized that the highest call to love is in loving the "unlovable." I also realized that I could be the one who is unlovable at times. That is a humbling thought for all of us to consider... The parable about the weeds and the wheat came alive to me, when it occurred that sometimes I am wheat, and sometimes I am weed. Please don't cut me down as a weed; I am wheat in the making! Or to put it another way, "God ain't finished with me yet!" It makes perfect sense that Jesus tells us that at the end, *He* will send his angels to gather the weeds for burning. A weed this morning might be wheat this afternoon. And then there is the other parable in Matthew 7:3 where I am told not to worry about my brother's *splinter*; rather, do something about the *plank* in my own eye! The way of humility...

These matters of the cross remind me of an old, tiny book about human relations which I read in my mid 20's, around the time I was experiencing profound spiritual conversion and attempting to re-order my life and priorities around new values. The author had said that the reason there is conflict in life is because where there are two people, pride drives each one to want to be right. The secret to having good human relations, he offered, was in trying to prove that the *other* person was right. This removed the tension barrier, and more often than not, the other person would then start trying to prove that the *first* person was right. Pretty soon, they realized they were both a little right and a little wrong, and could move on. But the key was in one person being willing to sacrifice pride in the name of peace and love. The lesson I learned: when conflict arises out of the pride to be right, start trying to prove that the other person is right. I love these one-liner truths for all ages that can be carried in the heart's front pocket!

The late Father Peter McCarthy, God rest his precious soul, was substituting in our parish one Sunday. Father McCarthy was known for his courageous sermons, which gracefully combined exhortation with gentleness. There was no skirting around truth. This particular Sunday, he was preaching on the subject of humility. He shared with us about Alexander Solzhenitsyn's book *The Gulag Archipelago*, in which the author reveals his discovery of God's existence and basically states that the fine line separating good from evil runs through the center of man's heart - *every* man's heart.

Now, *there* is a judgment filter to keep me humble...

My point in all this is that I am no more or less lovable in God's eyes - than my brother or sister. In fact, the more difficult the cross, the greater is the call to love. Jesus died for me, and I am a great sinner. Who am I to have to do less? If Jesus forgives my enemy for what she did to me, who am I not to forgive her? Like the weed and wheat scenario, sometimes my *friend* is my *enemy*... So the focus for me is not whether to forgive and to love, but how and why. "Why" has always been a driver for me in life... In loving Frank, the why was influenced by how he had loved me so unconditionally. But in another situation, distilled to its essence within my vocation, the why is simply "it's just the right thing to do." God will reward my obedience to His will with the grace to follow through. So the goal remains, getting it right about this thing called love.

C.S. Lewis' book, *The Four Loves*, distinguishes the four types of love as: affection, friendship, eros, and charity. More recently, Pope Benedict XVI's first encyclical, *Deus Caritas Est (God Is Love)*, draws us in faith to the truest form of God's unconditional love: agape.

In the book, *When Did We See You, Lord?* By Bishop Robert J. Baker, Diocese of Birmingham in Alabama, and Father Benedict J. Groeschel, C.F.R., we see excellent examples of situations where we are called to see and love Jesus in everyday society - starting right at home and in our own church and community families.

There is a tremendous call for mercy in today's society. Whether driven by self-righteous pride, envy, jealousy, fear, or some other motive, we often "look the other way" while the poor among us are ignored and neglected. Ironically and sadly, sometimes when faithful people do courageously answer the difficult call to love, they are persecuted by the "modern Pharisees" who pretend to be holy, giving "lip service" but, as in the parable of the Good Samaritan (Luke 10:25-37), refusing to see and/or respond to Christ suffering in someone right in front of us. Focusing on Christ's call, and strengthened by the Holy Spirit, the faithful must carry on the works begun by the apostles of the early church over 2000 years ago, loving and serving the Christ who is hidden in the least among us.

We are called to love our little brother in the womb who is "coming" and our little brother with dementia who is "going." These little alphas and omegas are truly the least among us, and are today's greatest call to love. I remember a taxi ride in Newark years ago, when the driver asked me if I was going to vote for a particular candidate who happened to support the right to abortion. As you can imagine, I expressed my thoughts on the matter…and then he began talking about rape, incest, etc. The only thing I could think of was the baby. When a baby is conceived, that's God's work. So I told him, "You know, the circumstances of one's conception have nothing to do with the value of their life. I have no idea whether you were conceived in the married love of your parents, or whether it was by rape or incest. It doesn't matter to me. You are a very special person, destined to take me to the airport at this very moment!" We both laughed. Who knows…?

Always the call of love is to the ultimate sacrifice of self for the good of another. In my commitment to love Frank, I had to be willing to die if it meant helping him on his own journey to God. And in so doing, I would be dying for love of God and ultimately for love of self.

It occurred to me on this journey that perhaps God came as a little baby so our hearts would be led to embrace him and care for him, as is the natural way of a mother for her child.

Had God come as the man Jesus, rather than as the baby, would we have embraced Him and found Love? If he had come as the man Jesus, would it have been possible to see past the man who looked just like us, to see Love and become as a child so as to enter the Kingdom of Heaven?

I wondered…could God be permitting the plague of dementia and Alzheimer's to exist so that we might be humbled in our "human bigness" and experience or witness the "becoming as a child" so that we might enter the Kingdom of Heaven? There is certainly much to ponder. Modern history reveals to us how the pride of earthly success is redeemed in the humility of sacrificial agape love.   Reflecting on the enormous and numerous contributions to society and to the church by President Ronald Reagan and Pope John Paul II, respectively, I have to wonder what God was teaching us, as we observed on the world stage, the mental and physical diminishment of these strong, wise, great men.   Truly, these giants became as little children. And the world was called to love them in their littleness, whether it was the mental "littleness" of President Reagan's dementia, or the physical "littleness" of Pope John Paul II's Parkinson's disease.   Each embraced and acknowledged their personal cross with humility and perseverance. Many times, I have wished I could speak with Nancy Reagan to learn from her personal experience of loving her "Ronnie" to the end. I saw her as a pioneer in embracing dementia, and she gave me hope and courage.

No one knows for sure the full meaning of the suffering in the world. But this I do know: in order to love Frank in his dementia, to give myself to him in care and sacrifice, I first had to walk in his shoes and know his pain.

What did Frank need from me? What could I give to him? This was my call to love.

What I learned is that Frank's spirit, his heart, and his soul were very much alive, while his brain and body were dying. When he could no longer talk, I would rest my head on his chest and listen to his heart beat for me. The gifts of a kiss, the squeeze of a hand - the knowing look in his blue eyes, were all signs of life and love within.

It amazes me that the world judges the demented person by what comes out of their mouth. No one but God and Frank himself knew for sure the level of life within him; I knew his *heart*... Consider that babies cannot speak at all, but they are very much alive. They feel hunger and thirst. They need to be held, kissed, fed and touched to grow. They need to feel warm and clean and safe. They need to be loved. I needed to love Frank the way I loved my grand daughter, Brantley. I had to love Frank and respond to him as my baby.

Realizing this profound truth gave new life to our journey. Frank was the Omega, Brantley was the Alpha. Jesus was in both of them calling me to love *Him*. Patience, kindness, gentleness - all the virtues we freely exercise in caring for a baby because we realize the baby cannot help itself. Neither can the demented person. Oh, how I prayed for patience! It is no longer possible for me to meet someone with dementia and not see the little person within. They are all precious. They all need us to love them.

On a humorous note, Frank would want to interject here that not *all* things about the care of toddlers and dementia patients are the same: for example, an adult's diaper is *not* changed by lifting their legs in the air...

Having embraced the truth of my husband's dementia and its call to love, I was still left with the mystery of "how" to do this. What follows are some of my personal approaches to "how," and are the result of trial and error while Frank was still living, combined with continuing prayer, reflection and contemplation since he died.

I learned that responding to the call to love is always situational and requires a blending of truth and love to produce faith and understanding. In other words, in recognizing the person's needs and abilities, and committing in my mind and heart to give of myself to meet their needs, I will be shown by God's grace, "how" to love. The marriage of man's free will or "fiat" to God's will - in the grace of faith and understanding, bears the fruit of agape Love. This truth was revealed to us by God himself when in Mary, he became "the fruit of her womb, Jesus."

I believe this loving Father of ours teaches in *every* moment, the spiritual lessons of truth and love, through examples of the physical world in *our present moment*. In loving us, God always meets us creatures where we are; to love Frank, I would have to meet him where he was. And I learned that the secret is in the heart. It means asking, seeking, knocking through the physical senses – then seeing, hearing, receiving through my heart. And it means *acting* with my heart. To act with the heart means entering into the other person's need and then responding to that need. Again, remembering the baby, sometimes we must even *anticipate* the need because it cannot be expressed; hence, we seek and find the unseen.

Simply put, it means living spiritually – with my heart – in a body and world which are physical. Wasn't this the original call of God to Adam and Eve? Thousands of years later, we still can't handle the prosperity of God's gift of truth and love, through His Word, His Spirit, and his very Presence in the Eucharist. Instead, we choose the road of pride by trying to figure things out and do things "my way". Ultimately, I have to get it right about this thing called love before I can spend eternity with God, Who *is* Love. I believe it is a lifelong learning in humility and gratitude.

Once during Frank's last year of life, our life between the rails, I was in a very low place. With baby Brantley asleep in the backseat, I drove to a lake for a period of quiet contemplation and rest. There was a yearning for my husband in my heart and in my gut which had been torturing me for some time. In my crying out to the Lord, I received His call for me to come into His Heart. Before, it had always been about asking Him to come into my heart. This was new. I desired to long for Jesus as my Spouse in the way I longed for my husband. I wanted to know Him more intimately in every way I could. Remembering the old adage that "absence makes the heart grow fonder", I thought that if I fasted from the Eucharist for a period of forty days, as Jesus had fasted from the people, that spousal longing for Jesus would be born in me.

Those forty days were a period of spiritual attacks. I had not discussed it with Father Angelus before doing it. Later, when I shared with him about it, Father reproved me (in love!) never to abstain from the Eucharist that way; that I needed the protection of His grace in the Eucharist now more than ever, as often as I could receive. But fortunately, the merciful Jesus blessed my faith and my ignorance; and on the fortieth day, which happened to be my birthday, He gifted me with the most glorious Eucharistic experience. It was a heavenly moment, embraced by Jesus Himself, waltzing to a celestial choir of angels above all the people – whose existence I was not even aware of in that moment.

That was also my last birthday with Frank. Before going to Mass that Sunday morning, I told Frank it was my birthday and asked him to sing "Happy Birthday" to me. He sang one line, and then drifted "somewhere else." It was a precious gift wrapped in sorrow. Perhaps the dance with Jesus was a signal grace of consolation to fill me with renewed faith, hope, love, and strength.

Even in dementia, Frank's spirit of loving and giving remained. But, unfortunately I did not always recognize it.

Once on Mother's Day, I almost missed the gift. My brother Rich and Frank and I were at the breakfast table when Rich wished me a "Happy Mother's Day." Frank asked, "Is today Mother's Day?" And then he ran back to his office at the other end of the house. Upon returning, he proudly presented me with one of his most prized possessions: a telephone company mug. My initial response was rather neutral and slightly cool; I had one just like it. The company had given one to every employee years earlier.

But then the light came on in my heart. What a lovely gift this was! Suddenly, I turned to Frank and said, "Honey, *that* is the most beautiful gift I've ever had. Thank you for giving it to me." The boyish smile, which accompanied his "you're welcome," said it all. I quickly jumped up, hugged him, and said, "Let's put some flowers in it so I can show it off to everyone who comes in our house." A bouquet of tiny silk roses turned that mug into the loveliest vase I have ever owned; and it still holds its place of honor in the den.

I had learned a very important lesson about hearts that day. But I still did not always get it right the first time. Once I had ordered a collection of video exercises with hopes that I could work on my physical health at home. On the evening of the day they arrived, I opened the box and scanned the contents. But too tired to read the directions, I left the box on the coffee table and Frank and I went to bed. The next morning, I excitedly went to read the directions – and the box was gone! Frank quickly denied all knowledge. After searching for an hour and finding pieces of literature here and there, but no tapes, my frustration turned into sobs of despair. Once again, my loving and kind hubby went back to his office. Upon his return, he reached out to give me his very favorite American flag necktie and asked, "Will this help?" Still sobbing, I blurted out, "No!" And then almost immediately I said, "Yes! Thank you, Sweetie." And then he held me until the tears were gone.

I found the tapes the next day, stuffed in a bookrack behind the world atlas... If it all hadn't happened just as it did, Frank might not have had the opportunity to express his love for me with his favorite necktie and a cherished hug, or to be thanked and praised by me. And I would have lost out on another very important "love lesson in the rain."

These lessons reshaped the "knowing" of our love for each other. We were first of all mature adult companions, soul mates equal to each other. Yet, there had always been times when I needed Frank to be my father figure, or he needed me to be his mother figure, but they were incidental and what we considered ordinary calls to married life. To us, the occasional role reversal was a normal part of a healthy marriage, because first and foremost we were best friends who respected and held each other in high esteem.   If I was a little insecure in the present moment, he rose to the father figure, and vice versa.   But even to the end, when our whole life existed between two rails and I was the mother, there were lovely moments of eye contact - that familiar knowing, which confirmed the eternal knowing. It was reshaped, but eternally present.

This brings to mind an important matter with regard to the nature of relationships at the time dementia arrives on the scene.   A friend in a situation similar to mine commented that her husband had been very difficult to live with their whole marriage. They stayed together because of their children, and now they were older. The fire of their love had sizzled long ago, and she resented the burden of his illness.   But later, I noticed she became more attentive to him and had a more charitable attitude about the situation. When I asked her how things were going, she told me that she realized she had to forgive him so she could be forgiven, and that he was helpless now. What fueled her compassion in her was remembering their early love years, and imagining she was holding their first child in her arms. She was then able to love him in a maternal way. It reminded me of when Brantley was a baby and I would hold her against my heart. The power of love that transcended our two hearts is indescribable. At times, I would think of my miscarried babies in heaven, and include each of them in our embrace, one name at a time.   It was beautiful, and I learned another lesson about the *healing* call of love.

Another situation involved a friend whose mother had Alzheimer's. Her mother had never been the nurturing type, and the daughter suffered from many psychological issues as a result. For one thing, healthy "mothering" had never been modeled for my friend, although she herself was a mother of two children. The requirement to care for her mother was met with bitterness and resentment, and somewhat of a "vengeance" attitude. It brought to mind the feelings of resentment I had when I was strapped with so many responsibilities at 16, when my dad died and left me caring for my mother and younger siblings. Then, as a young parent myself, I had to face my own imperfections. And then I better understood the imperfections of my own parents. Both of my parents were high-strung New Yorkers with strong personalities. The tension at times was overwhelming, so I would go outside and climb a tree and visit with the squirrels. I suppose my daughter and my sister that I raised had to have their trees and squirrels, too...

What was revealed in humble reflection of my own weaknesses and mistakes was that God made all of us humans perfectly imperfect! That gave me the ability to understand the faults of my parents, and forgive them, and to understand my own faults and forgive myself. I know that love is a gift, and the most necessary form of giving is *forgiving*. That means I have to forgive my parents in order to love them. I have to forgive myself in order to love myself. In the Lord's Prayer, or the Our Father, which Jesus Himself taught us to pray, we ask God to "forgive us our trespasses as we forgive those who trespass against us." Clearly, forgiveness is conditional. I give it and I get it. I don't give it, and I don't get it.

It seems that when I have trouble forgiving someone else, the best thing for me to do is go to that inner place where I can reflect on my own shortcomings. Then I realize that their shortcomings are no more or less than mine. Likewise, sometimes when I am too hard on myself, I have to remember I am human like everyone else, and forgive myself.

Forgiveness gives way to the "resurrection" of a dead relationship. All relationships go through periods of pain and suffering, and sometimes even death. But to give and accept forgiveness returns life - returns love - to the relationship. Otherwise, the relationship remains broken, dead.

It is interesting to ponder Jesus on His cross. "Father, forgive them, for they know not what they do." Is it possible that those words, representing Jesus' gift of love as forgiveness, were *required* for the resurrection to occur? Were those words spoken to reveal to us the action of His heart, to show us the *way* to resurrect love?

In practical terms, it certainly seems that this is what must occur for human relationships to be healed.

I don't know whether my friend ever forgave her mother before she died. But I do know that we all learn from what we live. There are lessons about love that we must all learn in this life, and the God of Second Chances will hound us till we get it right. Each new opportunity presented is a little more up close and in my face, so sooner is better... It became clear to me, when facing Frank's situation and the call for role reversal, that I had not handled my mother's depression and illness as charitably as I should have. The fact is, I did not know how, and I did the best I could with what I had to work with. But as I grew in my faith life and had a desire to serve God in His will, my defects became more obvious to me. And there always seems to be another opportunity for me to "get it right…"

Beverly, a lifelong friend who is a few months older than I am, has two grand daughters a little older than my two. Since our retirements, we have each been taking care of our girls several days a week. One day we were talking about school days, telephone company days, and our daughters. The fact is, both of us were career women and our daughters went to day care. As grandmothers, we are experiencing the life of stay-at-home mothers, which we never knew. We laughingly admitted that this was our chance to "get it right." We were born to be mothers, perfected in "grandmotherhood" through the love and mercy of the God of Second Chances! And both of us would admit that this job is harder than any position we held in our telephone careers, that it is more *important*, and that it is the most rewarding. We now have realized that this call to love babies in our retirement prepared us both for our calls to elder care.

It's not easy to respond with unconditional, agape love. This is especially true in dealing with dementia. Sacrifice is difficult, it's uncomfortable, and it hurts at times. Sometimes the fear is so overwhelming that we run from the obligation, and then justify our response by focusing on our loved one's faults. We cling to the pain they caused us, from their imperfect parenting, and it becomes our reason for abandoning our own call. Were we, are we, the perfect child? Quite frequently, one sibling is left to manage the care of the demented parent with little or no support from other siblings. Sometimes the parent gets little or no help from the children at all. The saddest of all situations I witnessed were those little people in "the club" who never had visitors at all.

They were missing the gift of forgiveness, which gives forgiveness back.

Sometimes the learning comes only through the perspective experience, i.e. where *we* are the one who is alone and helpless and no one comes to visit *us*. In that time of sorrow, objective reflection can help us realize that we had done to someone else what is now being done to us. I was visiting a 46-year old co-worker once who had experienced a debilitating stroke and was living in a nursing home with all elderly people. He had, for some reason, felt led to confess to me a memory he had of having been cruel to someone who loved him many years earlier. In his aloneness and fear, he had come to know and regret the pain and sorrow he had inflicted; and now he had a contrite spirit. I told him about God's love and forgiveness, and suggested he pray for his old friend each day. The next time I visited him, he told me he had discovered how he could help young people from his wheelchair, so he felt a new purpose with redemptive merit. I believe that was the fruit of his suffering; learning a new way to love and serve God by serving others, even in his limited capacity.

Everyone has God-given talents which enable us all to respond to His call to love within our vocation and work. Take for example, barbers and hair stylists. For years Frank had his hair cut at Gary's Barber Shop. But when Frank became bedridden, Gary came to our home several times and brought what was necessary to cut Frank's hair in bed. The sitter spread the towels, I held the vacuum, and Gary did the barbering. Gary shared his gift in love.

And there is my own hairdresser, Monika. For 25 years her salon, Blades, has been a place for excellent hair care as well as a place to be consoled in life issues. In fact, hair salons are expert networking places for that very reason; whatever the life issue, Monika – an excellent listener, or another client, could usually connect me with a support person. Case in point: one Saturday morning, I was editing the manuscript for this book while waiting for my appointment. Before long, Monika introduced me to another customer whose father had a rare form of dementia, and we began talking. Then others chimed in. Soon there was a group of ladies wanting to know how soon the book would be available, because someone they knew needed it. We were all learning from and supporting each other. We were all sharing our talents, our gifts, in love.

And so, I have learned that responding to the call to love is as unique as the two people, the two hearts, brought together by God in any present moment. I have learned "how" by embracing the needs of my loved one, and through the examples of others, like my late friend Al Propst who kept a daily list of people he would call - just to see if they needed any help. I was one of those people he called each day, and I miss him greatly. And I learned another great lesson from my "best friend Al Propst" *after* his death, when at his funeral I heard at least 50 *other* people say he was *their* best friend. His is an epitaph written in many hearts.

"When did we see you, Lord?"   The secret is in the two hearts. Jesus said, "Come and see." Let me watch, and see with my heart, even in darkness...

CHAPTER
EIGHT
♥♥

One Dark Lenten Night

Lent began for me long ago
"Fasting from my groom while he's still here"
It's not supposed to happen that way, no
But our Lord - THE bridegroom – willed it so

The pain I've lived these past few weeks
And especially these last days
Why has it been so lethal?
Why does my spirit, my heart, lack life and purpose?
Why do I not know God's presence?
Why can't I feel your love?
Any love at all?

Though the lone Adam had God all to himself
God said it was not good for man to be alone
And so He gave him Eve
He knew His creatures needed natural love
And He knew that His grace is sufficient
He knew the love of man and woman
Is His manifestation of the Trinity
Fatherly Love, parental Love
God's interwoven Love

I have known that Love and Its loss
My Passion and Death
Oh, where is my heart's resurrection?
I believe, but am sad-you-see

Father God, my father above
Won't you grant my heart healing grace?
That the memories I hold
Of the blessings I've known
May revive my poor heart and soul
There is nothing more we own

Please God!

©Ellen Marie Edmonds 2008

Chapter 8: **Pain and Darkness**

At times, life was not unlike a perpetual season of Lent.

Maybe that's how life is *supposed* to be…a regular cycle of denying self, growing closer to God, accepting His will and submitting our will to His will, then returning to our life duties balanced in His Love. Perhaps the church's annual 40-day Lenten period of sacrifice – and Jesus' own 40-day fast – were given to us by God to teach us the "little way" to peace through these periodic practices of self denial. It could be. Nevertheless, in the midst of heart-wrenching pain and darkness, even my strong faith sometimes seemed like a distant friend.

And one hot summer morning, the garden brought new hope…

As the lily blooms
In the hot summer drought
So His light shines forth
In the darkest night

Still, there were those moments so seemingly hopeless that I would cry out to God in anguish. Having journaled many of those desperate cries, I realized in retrospect how hope had sustained me through my knowing there was purpose in our suffering. Poor Frank's suffering; my own suffering; and then I would contemplate Christ's suffering, and that of his mother Mary who embraced His passion and cross with Him. Somehow in all of this, I would recall applicable Scripture passages which St. Paul had written that connected my sacrifice of love with Christ's sacrifice of love. The "why it matters" factor lifted my spirit, and would get me through the moment. But as Frank deteriorated and as I embraced his journey with him, those dark moments occurred more often.

Can you imagine being trapped in your own mind, by your own body? A dear friend of mine was losing her mother to dementia at the same time I was losing Frank. Courageously, my friend Peggy allowed herself to enter the pain and darkness of her mother's journey. She described her mother as being trapped in a dark forest, searching and seeking but never finding the way out. In a flash, she was trapped in a room full of people, all with faces she did not recognize. She was lost, and did not know which way to go... The close bond between mother and daughter was evident in the love my friend had for her mother, and her sensitivity to her suffering. I was quite touched by her compassion and her willingness to "feel" with her mother. In our pain-avoiding society, such empathy is rare. The exception might be with children, especially toddlers and infants.

When a toddler is among strangers, she may become frightened and seek out her mother or grandmother for security. Spotting her mother, or running to her arms, removes her fear and anxiety. It seemed this might work with Frank, as well. When Frank appeared to be lost, I would bring him into a place of familiarity with words or phrases or songs or prayer.

Sometimes just a hug would do it.   He would even "jitterbug" with me from his bed, with me humming an old swing song and him with his feet and shoulders dancing.   Even today, I treasure the memory of those dancing moments, which rare and simple as they were, rekindled the fire of romantic love in a darkening world.

As our world grew smaller and darker, it took very little to give us the light of joy. That tiny little flame lit our dark world with hope, with trust, with purpose, with eternal love.   And it seemed even sweeter than I had remembered. I am forever grateful for having known this fragrance.

I often wondered whether the pain and darkness was more of an experience for me than for Frank, because I was the one with the healthy memory and the ability to see the net loss of yesterday from today. For Frank, going backwards meant he was almost always in the "now." And the heart – where love resides – is the perpetual "now." So there was some consolation to me in realizing that the plus side of cognitive loss was the derived loss of emotional pain and fear. I can't be sure of this, but intuition tells me it's true.

Thinking about the toddler or the infant again, what would constitute emotional pain and darkness to them? I would say it is the fear of being alone, or in a strange place, or of being with strangers; or feeling a basic need such as hunger, wetness, coldness, etc. It seems to me the same fear-based pain would apply to the adult with advanced dementia, and so that assumption often guided the response to my husband's behaviors.

Reflecting on Frank's in-home care situation and the comfort he knew from familiar environs, I find solace in the belief that as my pain seemed to increase, Frank's level of suffering did seem to lessen, simply because his ability to reason diminished; sort of a blessing in disguise, if you will. I would go through that shift in suffering all over again, if it meant his pain was less and he could go in childlike peace. This understanding of my suffering as gift to Frank helped me endure and deal with the ever present reality of grief, which arrived long before his death.

CHAPTER
NINE
♥♥

F-R-O-Z-E-N

Layin' in the big bed
Necked as a jaybird
Freezin' from head to toe
Lookin' for my hubby and
Needin' him to hold me
Damn – where did he go?

Shivverin' down the hallway
Slippin' in my booties
Slidin' down the old stairway
Jumpin' in the little bed
Kissin' on his sweet head
Startin' a brand new day

Wakin' in my loneness
Searchin' for my wholeness
Day after day after day
Waitin' on the Tall Man
Take us to the Big House
Startin' a brand new Way

Layin' in the big bed
Necked as a jaybird
Freezin' from head to toe
Waitin' on the Sonshine
Hopin' for the big one
Just gotta let it go

©Ellen Marie Edmonds 2008

Chapter 9: Grief the Thief

Frozen, somewhere between married and widowed, I longed for the joy I had known, and struggled each day to find hope. *Enter*: grief the thief.

Undermining my accepting and embracing of Frank's dementia and our new life together was the dark drone of terrible grief over the loss of the person of my soul mate. My husband was physically present. True, I was Mrs. Frank Edmonds. But I felt like a living widow, caring for a big baby I dearly loved.   And like a baby, his interest was in basic needs; and there was no capacity to meet my needs. I was so alone, and no one seemed to understand my pain.   Normally, I am sensitive to the needs of others; but grief creates a numbness which often desensitizes us to the pain of others, even blocking it from memory. To those I may have insensitively offended during those dark days, I ask understanding and forgiveness.

The burden of grief associated with loss due to dementia is both excruciating and unpredictable. With heightened emotions, I was easily and frequently hurt by the littlest acts of omission.   Even those with superior coping skills can find themselves acting in ways which are out of character, as they struggle to cling to normalcy. Fortunately, there were a couple of very close friends who could recognize my difficulties; and they were committed to helping me through difficult moments.

True, there were support groups available with some particular benefits, but there was little help for grief. And grief groups I checked out did not deal with "anticipated grief." In anger, I had responded, "My grief is not anticipated - it is here - *now!*" And then I would find consolation writing in my journal...

There is an interesting dynamic that occurs within a family when dementia attacks. Often there is denial or fear or both. Our family was scattered about the country, so it must have been shocking to come once a year and witness the progression of Frank's illness. Contrast this to the family members and friends living nearby who visited regularly and saw the gradual progression. I suppose all of these factors play into the unique response of each individual to the reality of a loved one's dementia. The greater the love has been, the greater the pain will be. There is really no room for judgment in these matters except by God Himself, Who is the only one with full understanding of the situation. Nevertheless, sometimes my writing reflected a little anger...

Night time is my time
No time for you time
Shut it off
Shut you out
No time for you tonight time.
Night time, anytime
Always here for you time
Always on
Always in
Love I give to you time.
Night time, dark time
No time for you time
Turn it on
Leave it on
Always here for you time.

Suffice it to say that the pain and the grief are real, whatever the level; and it must be dealt with in healthy ways of mourning or it manifests in various forms of illness that steal our health – enter again: grief the thief.

136

Dr. Alan Wolfelt, an expert in loss and transition, has published many books on the subject of grief in many of its forms. While I have not yet seen a book specifically dealing with the grief of dementia - the dementia patient's grief as well as the grief of their loved ones, I am hopeful there will be more resources available in the future.

My own grief was indescribable; but the extent of Frank's personal grief is unimaginable to me. It is my hope that in loving Frank, and in allowing myself to enter into his suffering, assuring him of my presence, etc., that I was somehow able to help relieve some of his personal grief. I won't know that answer in this lifetime.

Often, I found myself writing love letters to Frank, poems in my journal, believing his heart would hear the groans of my heart...

On that day - the day of hearts ♥ ♥
Lovers share moments together
Giving gift of their time, of one to the other
Only one
Above every other
Unspoken bond of belonging
Two Hearts, one Love, one Life
...at least for a moment
So precious, if *only* a moment...
The Queen assured He is her King
The King, more sure than she
As he holds her close
As she knows his soul
Saying nothing – and saying all
Just being, just giving
Love
Day or night or night or day
Or even St. Valentine's Day -
The day? It doesn't matter...
Only the Lover Who really loves
Who gives till it hurts to the other
Pure love, God's love, their love
It matters

> The King so loved the Queen
> O' fragrant holy years!
> The King – he died
> The Queen – she cried
> O' bitter sweet tears
> Her valentine is dead
> And so she goes to bed
> And writes in this book of red

Amazingly, expressing my pain in "love poems" proved to be a therapeutic form of mourning – an *outward* expression of the *internal* pain which was most intense during that last year of Frank's life. I understand that many people, in the depths of grief, are unable to write or express themselves at all, but find healing in reading the written expressions of others. It is with that hope in mind that I share my writings with those who are suffering as I have suffered.

With regard to family and friends, grief manifested itself in a variety of ways. Surprisingly, many of the ones Frank loved most and longed to see stayed away. I have to believe it was due to their inability to handle the pain of watching him diminish and suffer. I have often heard that sick people seem to hurt the people they love most. Perhaps it's the reverse: sick people are hurt the most by people they love. Or perhaps both are true. Whatever the case, you can be sure that "grief the thief" steals away important relationships at the most inopportune time. As pervasive as dementia is in today's society, and as difficult as it seems to be for everyone involved, more help is certainly needed with this type of grief. A counselor told me that very often, people realize inhibited grief years after the loved one's death, mixed with feelings of guilt and shame. Dr. Alan Wolfelt's book, *Living in the Shadow of the Ghosts of Grief*, offers healing help for this type of grief, by first going backwards in order to move forward. This principle has been confirmed for me in the writing of this book, as I go backwards into the dementia journey and re-experience the pain; new levels of learning and understanding occur, which in itself brings healing.

With regard to *dealing* with my own personal grief, my "therapy" included seeking frequent spiritual direction and attending daily Mass when I could - before Brantley's mobile and vocal stage of independence! Each day began with a prayer of consecration to the Father, and ended in a prayer of exhaustion. I slept well. Two prayer devotions which I have enjoyed for years are the Rosary Prayer, which I tried to pray in the morning or at night, and the Divine Mercy prayer which I tried to pray at 3 PM – the hour when Christ died on the cross. Those two universal devotions were available to nurture me 24 hours a day, which meant even at 2 AM I could unite my pitiful prayer – or parts of it till I fell asleep – with all my brothers and sisters around the world who were praying the same prayer, or who were in a chapel somewhere adoring God. It was a healing tonic for loneliness. And there was EWTN television, also available 24 hours a day, which always seemed to have just the perfect message for me.

Dealing with my grief also meant humbly asking friends to spend time with me at dinner or a movie, etc., and taking an occasional weekend retreat to gather my wits and refresh my spirit. No one is a mind reader, and we aren't all as intuitive as some. It was important to be honest and open about my needs. One friend would frequently ask what she could do for me. But often, when I asked her to go have lunch or dinner with me, she declined. Finally, I responded to her offer by saying, "You know, I have to eat. If you will go with me to lunch, you can be sure that I eat. And we'll have time to talk." Later, she told me that she realized I was inviting her to meals because I needed her to just *be* with me; and this was the way she could help me most, by being present to me. And I thanked her.

Other ways I *unknowingly* dealt with grief was by helping people who were in difficult situations themselves. Sometimes it meant taking in someone who became homeless, helping with transportation needs, or simply adopting the lonely in Christ's love. For years, my husband and I had a special place in our hearts for priests. Through adopting them into our lives and our family, we were blessed to minister to priests in all stages of life: in seminary, newly ordained, new to our parish, leaving our parish, those with emotional and/or physical illness, and in pre- or post-retirement. There were a couple of priests with particular needs during the time of Frank's illness; we were all able to share our gifts to help each other. Ministering to fellow brothers and sisters in these ways often resulted in reciprocal graces which lightened the cross.

But the most effective method for me in *coping* with the grief of dementia was my journal. There were no boundaries, no time limits, no arguments, and no interruptions. I've never considered myself to be a poet, and aside from the Psalms of Holy Scripture and mandatory academic readings, I have never been particularly drawn to poetry. But having seen my own grief expressed in what became poetry, I have a new understanding of and appreciation for this type of writing from the heart. Mystical poetry is not the kind of thing you can simply decide mentally to write; it writes itself from within the soul, with a song all its own.

In my poems, I revealed to *myself* - and to the world, the brokenness Frank and I experienced from dementia, but also how God manifested Himself as the Light of our darkest night. Capturing this written expression of my grief allowed mourning, which is the healing of grief, to break through. Journaling let me feel. Feeling allowed me to heal. Even today, each time I read my own writings from that period of life, I am often humbled to learn some new truth about God and love and self and hope.

In the summer of 2002, I was asked to start a Rosary Makers ministry by our parish priest, Father John. Besides bringing the powerful Rosary Prayer, and also the Divine Mercy prayer which is prayed on the same beads, to thousands of soldiers, prisoners, homebound, and hospitalized, we made thousands for mission parishes in Alabama and around the world. Once, we shipped **3,000** rosaries to Africa for children who had requested them! By teaming up with other ministries in our church who helped fund our supplies and shipping, our team of men, women, and children were able to make with our hands and our love beautiful sacramentals to help others in their faith walk. The ministry and art form of rosary making is therapeutic in itself, and was a tremendous way of coping with my grief. And the graces received in return from this ministry are so immeasurable that we offer an annual teaching clinic to the public.

Another area of ministry which was unknowingly therapeutic on this grief journey was helping mothers in crisis pregnancy. The first lady I helped in this situation probably helped me as much as I helped her, particularly with Frank's care and in dealing with the sudden death of my brother, who was also her long-time friend. Asking me to be Godmother to her baby girl was a special joy of diversion all its own. Most significantly was how she prepared me for the birth of my own first grandbaby, through helping her with the birth of her baby three weeks earlier. It had been a long time since I had cared for an infant. In helping her during those first couple of weeks after her baby's birth, I received a crash course on labor, delivery, the hospital, nurses, infant formulas, diapers, immunization, pediatric care, infant seats, etc.; she even educated me on the use of digital cameras! When my grandbaby was born three weeks later at the same hospital, I was ready to go! In giving, I received; I was better prepared to help my daughter, and to grandmother our baby. And then along came Katrina.

Just a few months before Frank's death, Hurricane Katrina wiped out the Mississippi Coast, and my brother was left homeless. He lived with me for several months, as he tried to recover from this catastrophic event. Focusing on his needs and helping him get assistance was important for him. But it was also good for me to have my brother present, with his own special gifts, and to be with me after Frank died. We were there for each other at a time critical to us both. And it was another fruitful diversion from grief.

Helping others in crises certainly shed a different light on my own situation and lightened my cross a bit. But I believe that the stabilizer for me, for my sanity, was my faith and its certainty of hope. The gratitude I feel toward all those who helped form and feed my faith is enormous. Priests, family, friends, social workers, strangers, have all shaped my faith; but mostly I credit the Holy Spirit, because I know He is always there for me. Having a constant awareness of the presence of God within me, and my dependence upon Him for everything, keeps me humble and provides a constant framework of reference for making decisions and dealing with life. That doesn't make the pain go away, but it gives the pain meaning.

After Frank's death, I was invited by the Rev. Peggy McClure, Executive Director of Community Grief Support, to participate in a program just for the recently widowed. It was an excellent program of healing, facilitated by the Rev. John Harris, who encouraged me to continue journaling and ministering to other bereaved widows through writing. The program included excellent materials published by Dr. Alan Wolfelt, as well as the book, *Seven Choices: Finding Daylight after Loss Shatters Your World*, by Dr. Elizabeth Harper Neeld. I believe what was most helpful in the program was learning that those awful feelings of anxiety and confusion that I was experiencing were a normal part of widow grief and emotional exhaustion; that I was not crazy, and I would heal. Ah, the power of new hope! During the grief program for widows, Sharon Payne Hardy and I co-published a book entitled *Finding the Path to My Second Wind: Restoring the Heart after Loss*. It is a collection of grief poetry associated with anticipated death (my husband) and sudden death (Sharon's husband), and is linked to the "seven choices" of Dr. Neeld's book. Our book was privately published at the request of our grief work facilitator, hoping to aid others who have difficulty expressing their grief.

Another grief group I participated in was at my parish church, Our Lady of the Valley, under the dedicated direction of Sister Madeline Contorno, O.S.B. It was open to anyone who had experienced the loss of any loved one any time, and included the dynamic of a shared faith within the church family. Both grief programs continue to be a source of healing support and friendships; and the life lessons learned through these programs continue to guide and comfort me in a reciprocal way.

Truly, life is a series of responses to loss. Grief is a natural, internal response to loss. Learning healthy ways to mourn, or outwardly express my grief, has become as important to me as good nutrition and exercise.

For people who are facing the grief of dementia, the grief is as real – and maybe even more painful – than the grief from death itself. It is important to recognize its presence as soon as possible, and to employ a healthy coping plan. We call it "grief work." And then we continue healing through mourning - giving back, widows helping widows - as we have been helped.

WIDOW ANGELS

The painful blow of grief was yours
Not so long ago
The one you loved the most was gone
And you felt all alone.
Broken heart, your world so dark
Till HOPE came along
And shared its sorrow song
Through wounded hearts of yore
Who suffered this before
Yet somehow they did mend
And found their second wind
Through mourning ... evenings, too
Till FAITH came to you
And then it was your turn
To seek the hurting soul
Wounded, hopeless heart
Grief work was your goal
You shared what you had felt
When you were in their shoes
And how you learned from others
That you would have to choose
To live your life again
The old and new a blend
Transformed by God above
And friends who care enough
To give their gift of LOVE
As given them before
By other widow angels
Who entered through this door
A circle of friendship
FAITH, HOPE, LOVE
Sharing laughs and tears
Coping with new fears
Holding hands and hearts
With hugs each meeting parts.
Do you know that woman?
Have you seen her face?
When I fall she helps me up;
I think her name is GRACE.

©Ellen Marie Edmonds 2008

CHAPTER TEN

♥♥

JINGLE BELL BIRTHDAY

Jingle Bell Jitterbug
Birthday Boy Rock
Dancing and singing
Heaven's own clock
Heavenly jitterbug
Two dancing hearts
Baby and Angels
Love rocks the cart

Driving down '31
Babe's in the back
Santa and reindeer
Toys in a sack
Spirit of Christmas
Joy in the air
Birthday Hubby
Dancing to share

Jingle Bell Jitterbug
Birthday Boy – where?
Two lovers dancing
In the frosty air

©Ellen Marie Edmonds 2008

Chapter 10: **Humor the Healer**

Hopefully no one noticed us…

There we were, Brantley and I - with Frank in spirit - driving down the highway, laughing and dancing to one of his favorite Christmas songs: "Jingle Bell Rock"! It was Frank's favorite time of year: his birthday and Christmas time. This moment was his! He led our dance; I knew and kept his moves. We were, of course, invisible to all the passing cars busily making their way to shopping malls… The laughing and dancing – the silliness itself, felt good; it brought joy; and I believe our hearts were united with Frank's in that dance. All this was unbeknown to my friend Dawn, who surprised me that same evening with a heart shaped collectible ornament, depicting a jitterbugging Mr. & Mrs. Santa… God is so good! Later, I captured those sacred moments of humor and love in my journal, keeping it alive forever. Humor heals and love unites – wherever, whenever, forever. The lesson learned that day through Brantley, Frank, and Dawn: sometimes, we just have to let the little kid in us play.

Laughter can be a life saver! The mistakes I made. The behavior changes we experienced. The new "language" experience; observing Frank as an adolescent and teenager; these moments were truly funny, and it was important to let out the laugh! Frank had a great sense of humor, and he would want us to enjoy these stories and reap the benefits of laughter.

Often when someone with dementia can't find something, which they probably hid from themselves, they think someone stole it. A friend's father had a glass eye, which he would remove for sleeping. One morning he could not find his eye and accused his daughter of stealing it. Why would she want his glass eye? We both enjoyed that one. Fortunately, he had a lot of extras – but they were 1,000 miles away! So, until the eyeballs arrived, the old patch had to be worn. And that was another challenge...

Another lady told me about visiting her father at a facility, and something just didn't look right about his mouth. It turned out he was wearing someone else's dentures! This was funny, but it could have had serious health risks. I never heard how that one was resolved, though I wonder what was going on in the other patient's mouth.

One story I must tell in humility is about the infamous cinnamon roll, which everyone who knew me heard about... On a trip to the mountains, Frank and I had picked up breakfast including my favorite cinnamon roll and his favorite biscuit. I left the car for a moment, and when I returned my cinnamon roll (along with his biscuit) was gone. There was an empty box. There were no more cinnamon rolls available and breakfast was no longer being served. Like a child I lashed out and said, "You ate my cinnamon roll!" "No I didn't," he denied, rather sheepishly. "You are lying! You ate my cinnamon roll!" I yelled, a bit out of control.

This sounds silly, but little things like a cinnamon roll gave great joy – I felt robbed! When I settled down, I felt terrible for having yelled at him, even in truth. In that moment of repentance, I realized that if a toddler sees something he wants to eat, he thinks it's *his*! He eats it! Of course Frank didn't eat *my* cinnamon roll; it was *his*! I have laughed many times telling this story, which, on the serious side, was a huge insight and taught me one more lesson about the similarities to toddlers.

Another funny...when we were in a restaurant and soldiers in uniform were present, Frank had a custom of shaking their hands and thanking them for serving the country. One time he said, "I'm a World War II veteran myself." The soldier asked, "What did you do in the war?" And Frank quickly replied, "Man, I was dodging bullets!"

In honor of Frank's patriotism and heroism, and his life-long support of military men and women, I continue his tradition of thanking soldiers for so bravely serving our country.

Some experiences were painful, and I had to search for the humor. It was almost always there if I could just see the glass half full. The first day I dropped Frank off for day care, I was wrought with the concerns of a mother on her child's first day of school. After about an hour, I called to check on him. "Oh, he's doing fine," they told me. "He and Ms. Tyson have been holding hands and walking all around the building." It was bittersweet humor - my husband had a new girlfriend, and I had to laugh and praise his progress.

Frank always loved dogs, and toddlers love stuffed animals. So I bought him a cute little stuffed beagle puppy for his bed. We called him Barney, after one of his favorite old dogs. Barney brought Frank lots of comfort and pleasure. One day I asked about the pup, and Frank said, "You know, he never barks or runs off. He's a good dog." It was a good and funny experience.   And old Barney truly served an important role in Frank's happiness.

Speaking of animals, and remembering God's sense of humor... At the time when our cross seemed to be its heaviest, when pain was the greatest and days were their darkest, our God gave me brand new opportunities. On April 2, 2005, the day our sweet Pope John Paul II died, the young mother I had been helping, returned to the West Coast leaving behind two puppies, which were adopted by new families, and a kitten that no one wanted... In memory of Pope John Paul, I affectionately named the kitten "Lolak" which was John Paul's childhood nickname, and brought her home with me. Now there was Frank, my grandbaby and Lolak the kitten. In August, Hurricane Katrina hit the Coast, and my brother had come to live with me. One afternoon in September, my brother suggested taking tiny Lolak to the vet to determine her age and health; the cat was pregnant. I remember looking up to Heaven, laughing, and thinking, "Hey, thanks, Lord. I really needed some cats." The vet emphasized that her two kittens were very large, and their birth was overdue. Lolak needed a "nest" and we might have to help her deliver... Now *that's* something that doesn't happen every day. Later that night, I made a nest for Lolak in my closet. The next morning, she came into the bathroom with me, stretched out on the tiles, and proceeded to go in to labor. Having had little feline midwife experience, I prayed... Guided by faith, I pushed gently on her hind legs, and out popped the first kitty! Lolak moved quickly to her nest and proceeded with the birthing process. Meanwhile, a crowd had gathered in my bathroom to witness all this. Within about 20 minutes, the second kitty was born. And what did we name them? You guessed it - Alpha and

Omega! And of course, having delivered the first-born... and not being able to split the family... bonding had occurred. Cats? *Three* cats! In the middle of all these very serious "omega" life events, our God gifted us with feline "alphas" to refresh us in His humor. And it worked! Frank, Brantley, my brother, friends, all who visited our home were touched by these cute little fur balls. We delighted in watching them play and grow, providing a much-needed healing break for us all. Eventually, Lolak and the boys were old enough to live outdoors – and old enough to be modified... They developed keen hunting skills, enabling them to proudly surprise us with birds and moles and other such critters on the front porch. I reminded myself of what Frank would say about those critters: they are *gifts* for us from the cats! Just like the cats – all three of them - are *gifts* to us from God, I suppose. Hmmm...which type of *giving* would that be?

There are many more funny stories, which I won't share with the world, but which I cherish and still laugh about. A good humor rule of thumb: expect the unexpected. As with a toddler, someone with dementia might do anything - anywhere - any time. Keep it in perspective, deal with it, and then chuckle!

Humor is, indeed, a great healer. And God has a great sense of humor. So enjoy the funny side of the ride!

CHAPTER
ELEVEN
♥♥

HEALING RAIN

Healing rain is falling down
I'm not afraid
I'm not afraid
Let it rain
Heal the pain
Let it fall
Heal it all
Healing rain is falling down

Fragile heart - -
Weary soul - - -
Broken spirit - - - -

Healing rain is falling down
Be not afraid
Be not afraid
Let it rain
Take the pain
Let it pour
Care no more
Let it fall
Take it all
Healing rain is falling down.

Falling down…

©Ellen Marie Edmonds 2008

Chapter 11: Family, Friends, and My Journal

The invasion of dementia into our lives was not unlike an unannounced catastrophic tornado, ripping through the heart, the soul, and the spirit. Tearing down all in its path, it set a new and endless depth standard for the term "falling down." Down? There was no bottom.

If storms bring out the eagles – those strong, courageous birds that, with full confidence and trust, seek and embrace howling winds and torrential rains -   then it's fair to say that crises bring out true friends. Or maybe they weed out the enemies. Whichever the case, clearly there are those faithful family and friends who rose to the occasion to support Frank and me, and who made tremendous sacrifices within their own vocations to help us in our time of need. If in a lifetime we have known even a few true friends, courageous and willing to actually live the commitment of *philia* love – that love of friendship we can truly trust in good times and bad – we are most fortunate.   By the grace of God, I have known such friendships.

"Dawn of the Valley" as I call her, is always assisting the sick and dying. When I was facing my own mortality, she brought Communion - the Eucharist - to me daily. During Frank's illness, she visited our home faithfully. And one Memorial Day when Frank was living at "the club", she and her two teenaged sons gave up their holiday to bring their friend, Mr. Frank, a patriotic party. It was complete with cupcakes, balloons, and a game of "volley balloon" with Mr. Frank. They delighted him with festivity and honored him with their gift of self and friendship.

My friend Lynn was always taking the tough jobs, like spending the night with me at the hospital. True to her nature, when one of my sitters left suddenly during Frank's final days, Lynn came and spent the night with me to comfort me, but also to help me care for Frank until our other sitter arrived. She was a lifesaver, and I cherish her friendship. With Lynn nearby, I knew I could get through the night. Ours is a reciprocal trust.

Friends were amazing! Dedicated Beta Sigma Phi sorority sisters came through for me. Prayer group sisters and brothers lifted me in thought and prayer. Our Rosary Makers family, fellow Franciscan missionaries, Regnum Christi sisters – all gave of their hearts, their time, and their talents, making sacrifices to lighten our pain. God bless them abundantly!

Many co-workers and neighbors also offered to help, and I learned to say "yes" and "thank you." It is difficult, even for family, to visit with someone on their last walk of life, and it is truly an act of love. In fact, one of Frank's grand daughters gave him a loving gift of song and touch on his last Sunday morning; I believe her gift of presence helped Frank be able to go in peace just a few days later.

My daughter Shayne gifted her "Big Daddy" with regular hugs. But her greatest gift to him, to us, was the presence of little Brantley, who brightened each new day for us, and would sit on "Grand Daddy's" bed smiling at him, and bringing him the joy of new life. And Frank would look at her with her little bald head and say, "He's so cute!" Frank and Brantley had a deep understanding of one another... Shortly after Frank had died, I was copying a photo of him at Wal-Mart. His picture came up on the screen and I said, "There's Grand Daddy." Amazingly, Brantley looked at him and said, "Franklin. Franklin. Franklin." No one called him Franklin except his Big Mama. Brantley only knew him as Grand Daddy. Or did she? Could this have been a promised "signal" grace - a physical manifestation of a spiritual gift - from my little "Alpha" to my beloved "Omega," to console me? I still ponder this mystery.

And there were other special friends who came around. Because Frank was a war veteran and a Civilian Aide to the Secretary of the Army, he was provided with a Casualty Assistance Officer, Colonel Leonette Slay. Frank had always wanted to replace his war medals, which had been stolen years earlier from his home in Mississippi. This was arranged and fulfilled by Colonel Slay and General Darden in a bedside ceremony, surrounded by our closest friends and family, just a few months before Frank's death. Frank and I are forever grateful for the Army's quick response to me and for help arranging his military funeral locally and his burial at Arlington. Frank lived and died a proud *soldier*.

While friends and family were most important, their ability and/or willingness to listen and be present was naturally and understandably limited by their own life duties. When Father Palmer introduced me to journaling, I had no idea what a spiritual companion it would become. There was tremendous relief in being able to express anything - anger, sorrow, frustrations, and fears - without burdening anyone, with no arguments, no time limits, and no filters. Inevitably, God would reveal Himself to me in a subtle and gentle way. To this day, I continue that form of written contemplation and spiritual learning.

Loving family, friends, and my journal: each one held up a piece of our cross.

CHAPTER

TWELVE

♥♥

AS THE TREE…

Good morning, Father
Thank you for this day
Won't you please take my hand
And show me the way?
To walk in the valley
To climb the highest hill
To swim amidst the raging sea
Oh, Lord – to do your will

And He said, "My child
See the tree
See its roots planted firmly within the earth
See it change
With the storms, with the seasons
And with the rains
Always to serve Me
Always to glorify My will
Oh, pray, child
To be as the tree."

©Ellen Marie Edmonds 2008

Chapter 12: Help! Searching for Sitters

Trees are a great teacher of humble obedience to God's will. Have you ever thought about the stories they could tell, just standing there along the road for years and years, breathing in the carbon monoxide of passing cars? "Be still, and know that I am with you."   And He knew the groaning of my heart. Finding good sitters was definitely an answer to humble, perhaps even *pitiful* prayer, and the grace of God – for it came almost like manna from Heaven.

Father Richard had told me that the best care for Frank would be from family members. But when that was not possible for us, God blessed us with others to do the job. I learned that there are dedicated people called "sitters" who have a special gift of caring for the sick and elderly. Some sitters are also trained nurses. With the various stages of dementia, sitters were needed for different types of service – occasional sitting in my home; daytime sitting at the facility which we called "the club", and finally, live-in sitting in my home.

I learned there were a number of sitter services available, as well as private sitters. Local hospice and Alzheimer's organizations sometimes had sitter information available. And some churches offered free sitter service by volunteers. Fortunately, I had met an experienced sitter early on, who was connected to a network of sitter services, which was a lifesaver to me.

In my early search for help with Frank, I discovered sitters who would come to my home, and companion Frank while I was away, while doing light housework for me. Thinking they were my new "housekeepers" Frank was comfortable with their presence and maintained his sense of dignity and respect. Occasionally, a sitter would take Frank on outings or to lunch, which he enjoyed. The service allowed me to grocery shop and run errands, but it was still difficult to manage the affairs of our home because, like a toddler, he demanded or required my constant attention.

Sitter service was expensive, as all long term health care is; but it was not as expensive as the local nursing homes. And our in-home nursing option during the last 18 months provided us all – especially Frank - with the highest quality of care and quality of life. And it gave me peace of mind.

When nursing care is needed and in-home is not an option, a skilled nursing home may be necessary. As with all trials, we have to pray for guidance and do the best we can with what we have to work with. God will honor our response to His call to love. Knowing that we have sought God's will, and have done the best we could in love, we have to leave the rest to Him and be at peace.

CHAPTER

THIRTEEN

♥♥

LOVE LESSONS IN THE RAIN

If you like, you may hear My voice
Between the drops of rain
If you look, you may see My face
Holy, crying in your pain
If you listen, you may feel My heart
Bleeding in your wounds of love in vain

Arrows pierce the heart that beats for Love
Eros breaks the heart without My Love
Quakes - and darkest winter rain comes down
And in My Glory grows your springtime crown

Fragrant hope sweetens all your rain
Lessons of Agape – none in vain
Heaven's Heart eternal is your gain
From Love lessons in the rain

In my Love forgive your winter pain
Again, again, again – forgive the pain
Remember no Agape is in vain
All done for Me is not in vain

You have known a Love like Mine on earth
Rarely seen or known – Grace was birthed
Because your love was always for the other
Perfect love as for Me from my mother
Almost…
Always there for the other heart
Never desiring to be apart
From one you love
Who needs your love
Whose love you need
Always giving – to the other
Always loved – by the other
And loving
And there is where My Love is purest
True friendship; eros, philia, agape – gift

You have known this Love and you are blessed
He loved his wife like Christ loves His church
And even His church must have her Passion
Loved by Jesus Christ Himself

©Ellen Marie Edmonds 2008

Chapter 13: "The Club"

The pain of committed love bears great fruit in the form of life lessons, or "love lessons" if you will. These "rainy" moments of learning often came in the everyday care at home. And although there were many good experiences with facility care, there were also some particularly painful lessons learned.

Early in Frank's disease, a friend told me about an assisted living facility that offered day care for dementia patients. Frank had been talking about "going back to work", and so I visited the facility and asked if he could come as "a consultant" whose job was to interact with the people who lived there. They were excited about this program approach, so we tried it. On his desk in the library of "the club" was placed a sign, which said: "Frank Edmonds-Retired CEO and Consultant." Frank took pride in his "new job" and told many of our friends about it. He had a new sense of purpose. The appearance of the facility was a significant factor in its being selected; I knew Frank wanted nothing to do with nursing homes. But this place looked like a country club, so we called it "The Club".

This was the place where Frank met his new "girlfriend." He made lots of friends, enjoyed the meals and snacks, and was positively influenced by the environment and decor. It was a courtyard style facility, so it seemed safe and provided a lot of walking area, inside and out, with access to a lovely garden and gazebo. Weekend respite was available, where he could spend the night, if I needed to get away or just take a break. Those were the weekends he had a "business conference."

I was pleased with the day care service, and had used their services for about five months when a room became available for Frank. I did not know where we were going with his illness, but I knew he needed to be in a safe place and cared for by competent staff. It so happened this was also when my grandbaby was about to be born. I was also helping a mother in a crisis pregnancy, whose baby was due any day. Frank was able to stay day and night at "the club" during these two events, which was most helpful. It was very, very difficult for me not being able to see him during that time, but the staff recommended no visits during this "break-in" time for him. I'm still not sure what I think about that; he must have been at least as lonely and insecure as I was, and I had the advantage of knowing what was going on. It breaks my heart still to think of the fear he must have known at times. Little Riley would be terrified by something like this. Even I would be affected by such a change. I simply did what they told me I had to do. And it is important not to judge myself harshly with the wisdom of today, for what occurred yesterday within its own wisdom. Hindsight is always 20/20. It was a journey into the unknown, guided by love. In that, I am consoled.

A funny story must be interjected here. While staying with my daughter after her baby was born, I received a call from Frank at "the club." He was upset because they woke him at 6 a.m. to give him a shower, and they told him it was at my direction. He did not want a shower that early. I said, "Well, Sweetie Pie, I'm sorry that happened. I'll see what I can do to fix it." He responded, "They better do it. And I - am - not - your - sweetie - pie!" Clearly, I had been chastised…and the problem was corrected!

No one ever loved me the way Frank did. The pain of his absence, though he was still alive, is indescribable. It was heartbreaking going to bed at night alone, knowing that my husband was in another bed ten miles down the road - alone. I knew he needed me to be present with him. We needed to hold each other. That's what we did every night before going to sleep, and every morning upon awaking. My heart ached for and with him almost unbearably. Every night soaked my pillow and puffed my eyes. After just a few days, I realized I had to hold him each night until he fell asleep; then I could go home and go to sleep. It's what I had done with my daughter. It's what I was doing with my granddaughter. He was my baby, and his heart called for me.

I began going to see him every morning when he woke up, and then I picked up my grandbaby. In the evening I took the baby home, and stayed with Frank till he fell asleep. He thought we lived at "the club", and that I was at work during the day. Then I would go home, sleep, and do it all over again the next day. Day after day after day… and I would pray, "Give us this day our daily bread."

I frequently spent the night with Frank. With every visit, I brought a meal for us to eat together, in addition to his regular meals. Many of the "kids" who lived there saw me everyday, and thought I belonged to them. I got to know them all by name, gave and received hugs and kisses, and brought them treats. It was my preference to do his laundry and change his linens, so I developed several friendships with these "little people" in the laundry room.

One day a precious little lady resident I'll call Miss Edna, all dressed up and carrying her purse, came in the laundry room frantically searching for her mother. I asked her, "What does your mother like to do?" She told me her mom loved to sing in the choir at church. Then I told her, "I'll bet your mother went to the church already so she can sing." She was so happy! It was amazing how easy it was to console these grieving little ones simply by listening to their hearts and responding with compassion. Many points of understanding were gained from direct interface with these little people.

There were also many scientific points of understanding that I gained from a dementia seminar I attended after Frank's death. It seems the brain has a "heart-like" portion, which controls emotions and lives the longest in a dying brain. Often, at "the club" when there was no observed speech at all among some of the little people, there was still prayer and song, dancing and laughing. One old gentleman, I'll call Mr. Willie, never spoke; but he beautifully played "the club's" piano all day long! The music center of his brain was alive and well.

I am reminded of my mother's brother who had suffered a stroke. Uncle Billy had always been one of my favorites. When I visited him, he could not speak much, so he drew pictures to express himself. When I would "get it" he would say "right on!" But amazingly, when I told him I *loved* him, he clearly said, "I love you, too" with a great big smile. Like Mr. Willie, he was a musician and singer, and never missed any of the words. Despite cognitive disability, affection and singing brought him joy and new life.

There seems to be more to this brain and heart connection. I heard recently that science has discovered brain-like neurons located in the heart. If the brain has a "heart" and the heart has a "brain" there is much to ponder about the relationship between God's grace and my free will. How could I or anyone know these things, observe these little ones, and question the existence of our God?

There was one gentleman at "the club" in his late 60's, who I'll call Bobby, who never spoke - unless I asked him about his horse. His wife and I were friends and befriended each other's husband. She had told me he loved his horses. When I asked about his horse, his face would become radiant. When I asked the horse's name, he would be transformed into a precious little boy; and with a glowing smile he would say, "Sugar Foot." In those rare emotive moments, he would then describe her to me. Talking about his beloved horse gave him joy and new life. My gift was to ask him.

Those precious little people were everywhere just waiting to matter. One little lady I'll call Miss Maggie cried out "help" from her bed every time I passed her room on the way to Frank's room. In the beginning, it made me uncomfortable and I would hurry past. Then one day after her cry, I stopped and asked, "Lord, what is it You want me to do?" Then I went into her room. Her hair was straggled, her tiny face unwashed, and she was on a floor mattress so as not to fall from bed. When I put my hands on hers and looked into her pale blue eyes, I said, "Hello!" And she gifted me with the loveliest smile! "Thank you for being kind to me," she said. Can you imagine being so happy because a stranger came in and acknowledged you exist? I went in her bathroom, got a warm washcloth, and gently washed her little face. Upon inquiring with the staff about Miss Maggie, I was told she had cancer with little time left. She had been put in a room by herself, and probably suffered immense loneliness. Never did I see anyone with her, not even staff. It was as if she had been cast aside as already dead.

A few weeks later I noticed Miss Maggie walking the halls in her walker. She had been moved to a new room and was no longer alone. Thanks be to God! She had a miraculous turnaround, and was still there when I took Frank home a few months later. Only God knows when someone is truly dying. My job is to love them, even unto death.

One unforgettable event taught me a most significant lesson about dementia and about love. As I approached Frank on one of my regular visits to "the club", he began sobbing with his head in his hands. "What's the matter, Honey?" I asked. "I've lost all my wisdom," he cried out. My heart was pierced in a way I had never known. Quickly I said, "Well, Honey, you have not lost ANY of the wisdom of your heart. And I haven't lost my wisdom yet, so I'll share it with you." In a desperate hug of gratitude, he grabbed me in his arms and sobbed a hope-filled "Thank you."

I never forgot for one minute the reality and probability of those lucid moments. When they occurred, they must have been a horrific pain, a living death. As long as I lived, I would constantly remind him of my presence, my help, my love, my strength and my promise to share it all with him. It was the very least I could give to the one who loved me so unconditionally; yet, it may also have been the most he could give me.

What I could give Frank, even though he was living at "the club" was outings to our favorite restaurants. At least three times a week, I would take him out to eat, or eat with him in the dining room. He seemed quite happy with the fanfare, almost as if we were on a vacation; yet it was still somewhat like our every day life had been. Also, this was for me sort of a weaning process from the way things were to the way things were not. I still needed him in my life, and hung onto as many of the shared pleasures as possible, as I learned to adjust and accept life without my husband.

The lessons came rapidly and regularly, if I would but watch and listen with my heart.

As the brain dies, the person often becomes combative. My personal feeling about this is that it is an expression of anger rooted in the pain of fear and loss of their person. Compare this with the behavior of a toddler suffering separation anxiety when left at day care by his mother. I observed this in Frank, and with many other residents at "the club." The response of "the system" is to drug the patient so they are less anxious and easier to manage.

At the same time Frank's behavior was changing, conditions at "the club" had begun to decline significantly with a change of staff. The facility required Frank to participate in a geriatric psychiatric evaluation in a hospital environment in order to determine what "behavior medicines" were appropriate for him, and this was a condition of his staying in the facility. He had to leave immediately and could not return until the evaluation was complete and the facility re-accepted him.

This ultimatum was told to me on Friday morning of the 4th of July weekend! In my opinion this was completely inconsiderate of the patient and the family, extremely poor and incompetent business management by the staff, and it caused grievous pain and stress to my "little" Frank and to my whole family. With a 30-second unexpected directive, our lives and our support system were shattered. You see, my daughter was returning to work from maternity leave the following week, and I was to start keeping my 2 month old grand baby. But now a cloud of uncertainty had come upon us. Frank would have to be at a hospital, 30 miles away, undergoing who knows what type of traumatic evaluations, for an unidentified length of time.

"Whatsoever you do to the least of my people, that you do unto me." Those were Jesus' own words to us.

They wanted me to take Frank right then. I remember through sobs asking if he could stay a few more hours while I frantically searched for a church day care center which might be able to care for my new grand baby for a period of time. Finally, a sweet saintly lady named Clare heard my pain and gave me hope. On that same day began Frank's true passion and my personal walk in the shoes of our Mother Mary.

Due to falls at "the club" Frank had difficulty getting up from chairs or the floor, or getting out of the car, and he could no longer execute the stairs in our home. So I took Frank that night to our place where the crisis pregnancy mother and her new baby girl were living. The mother was a very strong young lady and had graciously offered to help me manage

Frank's mobility, etc. The next morning, Frank and I picked up our friend Al, who had offered to help me with the hospitalization opportunity...

God bless that angel in Heaven, Al Propst. The image is as fresh today as it was then, of Al pushing Frank around in a wheel chair, while I tended to admission matters. As they passed the window, Frank caught a glimpse of me sobbing profusely and yelled, "Ellen, is someone picking on you?" He was still protecting his Ellen. This was the hardest thing I had faced yet in our journey. My heart was completely shredded from the pain and guilt of subjecting Frank, who was now my little boy, to the harsh world of "business as usual" facilities which seemed to rarely employ enough compassionate and/or competent people. And *he* was concerned about *my* tears. My hope came in trusting that our merciful God would reward my compassion for strangers by sending compassionate strangers to minister to Frank in my absence.

It is important to note here that I also was constantly aware of the redemptive merit of our personal passion journey, i.e., uniting our suffering with that of Christ on the cross. This was our cross. Difficult as it was, meritorious as it might be, it could not compare to *the* passion of *Jesus*. When our cross seemed particularly heavy, that relativity - guided by faith and reasoning - became my greatest consolation and balancing rod.

Ten horrific days passed. I was only able to be with Frank in the evenings, when he was heavily drugged. Complaining that this arrangement was of no value to Frank, and asking for morning visits so as to help him, did no good. It was denied. There may be a perfectly logical reason for inflicting such a nightmare on a poor little soul, but I doubt it; rather, I think it is due to a lack of knowledge of what is really happening to the patient. No one would tell me what was being done to him, given to him, or when he would be released. His head hung down, he rarely ate, and the drugs given to him made him completely incontinent. (What a surprise that was for "the club" when he returned...) It was a nightmare from Gethsemane; I could almost feel the painful sweating of blood.

Everywhere on that floor were people in the same boat. One little lady I'll call Miss Helen, sat in a geri-chair in the TV lounge, and appeared to be laughing loudly almost all the time. As I tuned in to her, I realized she was actually crying hysterically. Her face reminded me of what my mother might have looked like if she were still alive. Drawn to her, I said "hello" and smiled at her. She stopped crying, smiled back and immediately asked me my name. When I said "Ellen", she said "I have a daughter named Ellen." This was bizarre. I wondered.... And the love lessons continued.

Eventually, my pastor intervened and helped get Frank released. Then it was back to "the club" complete with his new behavior medicines - and his new diapers.

As I expected, "the club's" response to this new call, to care for a 6'4" man in diapers, was met with resistance. I insisted they be respectful to Frank and use terms of dignity, such as "britches" or "shorts" rather than "diapers." While there were some very special and caring staff members there, I witnessed all too often a lack of respect in tone and language. Did they think these patients could not hear? Did they think the patients could not feel the sting of shame and humiliation from such language, especially when they knew that the emotive part of the brain was last to go? Or was it simply a lack of knowledge? Perhaps it was some combination of each.

In mercy, I knew I was called to love these staff people, too. Surely it was a lack of knowledge, staff support, funding or something at the root. No one would intentionally mistreat little ones, just because they were big, would they? As I discussed these matters with others, it became apparent that my thinking was with the heart, and was way outside the box. It seemed that, generally speaking, people working in dementia care were just a few steps ahead of most of society in trying to understand and respond to this pervasive brain disease. Everyone was doing the best they could with what they had to work with. It was my job to love them and not to judge them. We had to help each other through this mystery disease.

Life for us became more difficult at "the club", as you might imagine. It is difficult for small people to provide physical care for large people. I personally tended to Frank's hygiene needs when I was with him, but usually had to call for help. In a short period of time, however, he had lost 50 pounds from walking endlessly and not being fed. I popped up during lunch occasionally to discover him not in the dining room, but in his recliner which he could not get out of alone. His lunch tray would be sitting on a nearby stand which he could not reach. Go figure. His appetite was quite healthy if he could just reach the food! But the fact was, with the rapid weight loss, requiring more but getting less staff care, Frank was failing to thrive. My twice-a-day visits were not enough.

One day seemed painfully not unlike Calvary, as we slowly shuffled our way to his shower. My once strong and handsome husband, who had stood 6'4" and 240 pounds, could now barely walk with his boney legs. His drawn face showed the pain he bore from his broken lumbar, and who knows what else. His shoulders were pointed, and his arms limp. His ribs could be counted – even the extra one he had. And there in that moment I recalled the words of David the prophet, "They pierced His hands and feet; they numbered all his bones." And then my heart went to Mary. Oh, my God! What pain she felt – I felt - seeing her child, Jesus – my child, Frank - on that walk to death. The desire to help him and the pain of helplessness overtook me. I wanted to kiss him and make it better. Everything stopped. I could only hold him. And we both wept.

In the shower, I noticed his toenail was black. I wondered if anyone in the facility ever looked at him the way I did. Did anyone *see* him, I wondered? Did they see the helpless, sick, dying baby with their *heart*? Or did they see with their eyes only, a skinny old man whose chart had to be worked each day to keep the regulators happy and the budget balanced? I don't know. I have to believe the caregivers are simply understaffed and/or perhaps uneducated. Whatever the case, aside from the call to love there is an issue of basic human care that needs to be recognized. And as I understand from friends with similar experiences, this issue is not unique to "the club."

And then there was the breaking straw. Early one morning I cut through the courtyard to bring breakfast to Frank in his room. There, lying in the damp grass was my sweet hubby. He could have been there for hours, I don't know. Helpless and unable to get up, he just laid there. I ran to him, and not being able to lift him myself, called for help. It shocked me how many staff members walked past us and never offered to help. It angered me that it took 15 more minutes for someone to help us. Perhaps it was providential that I carried my digital camera with me all the time and thus captured a thorough and accurate account of these events. An interesting point is that when I reported this incident to the facility's director, she told me from his records a totally false account of the incident, which made it appear that Frank had been walking through the courtyard with me when he fell. This was completely untrue, and a matter of cover up and/or incompetent communications. The director refused to correct the record! It occurred to me that if they would fabricate a false record about an event that I personally experienced, what else would they do? Was he receiving real care, or were records just being noted? Again, this is not an arbitrary judgment but rather a legitimate observation and grievance question.

Later that night of the courtyard incident, I came to see Frank and he was no where to be found. Frantically, Bobby's wife and I searched inside and outside, to no avail. After insisting that the staff check inside a locked vacant room, I found my precious Frank sitting on the floor near the door, but unable to get up by himself. He had not been at dinner. Did anyone even miss him? How long had he been in there? Did he wander in or was this punishment? This was completely unacceptable.

Of course, the next day the director insisted that I get a full time sitter for Frank or move him to a nursing home. After sharing my concerns with a nurse friend from church regarding this recent "club" experience, Frank's diminishing physical health, and my feelings of anxiety and helplessness, it was suggested I bring hospice into the picture. The God-sent caring folks from AseraCare Hospice changed everything.

A week later, my older brother died of a heart attack in California. As I was making arrangements for his funeral in Mississippi, our dear friend Al died suddenly. Al had visited Frank that morning and fed him - you guessed it - a cinnamon roll! Two of my strongest supporters were suddenly *gone* in an instant. Pain turned to anger. And in my bedroom, I looked up to God - as if the ceiling weren't there - and yelled out, "CAN YOU CUT ME SOME SLACK DOWN HERE???" Then, feeling somewhat relieved, I got out my journal… I had to stay strong for Frank and Brantley.

This project, "Embracing Dementia - A Call to Love" is my compassionate attempt to help those patients and workers in dementia care facilities such as "the club", members of licensing boards, sitter services, and families with demented loved ones learn from my own experiences with Frank's journey. It is my hope that it will result in a better understanding of ambulatory patients as "big toddlers" and the bedridden as "infants;" and subsequently, through better education, provide safer and more effective care for these little ones with dementia. A self evident truth is that we all grow older and eventually die. What goes around comes around, and everyone's turn is coming. No better call for the Golden Rule have I witnessed!

Those of us caring for demented adults must remember that they are not capable of protecting themselves, or making good decisions, etc., any more than a baby or toddler is. Reasoning, sequential thinking, ordinary survival skills of an adult are not the same with dementia. For example, placing water fountains throughout "the club" was not adequate for keeping the patients hydrated; they forgot how to drink. Even putting a cup of water by the bed was not adequate. And with the disease progression, it often becomes necessary to help them put the cup to the mouth at regular intervals to maintain hydration. The same is true about food; I often had to help my husband lift the fork or sandwich to his mouth, until the point where he could no longer feed himself at all.

Before the auto accident Frank was in excellent health. He typically kept a glass of water with him and ate healthy foods. In the early stages of his disease, I noticed he rarely had a glass of water and only seemed to eat or drink something when I offered it. If there was food or drink on the counter, he would partake. In other words, the emotion of hunger would respond to the sight or offer of food, but his brain would not tell him "fix a sandwich" or "get a glass of water."

Remembering that the brain is going backwards to infancy, I learned it is best to use a schedule to be sure they get necessary nutrition, as with an infant. The same goes for incontinence; checking regularly keeps the patient clean, comfortable, and healthy. And just as important as the basic care requirements is their need for kindness and respect as a human being.

In a facility like "the club" caring for dementia residents required a caregiver-to-resident ratio similar to what would be required in a nursery or preschool for babies and toddlers. To allow a ratio of 1-to-12, as existed at the time in "the club," made it impossible for the workers to respond to the needs of their residents. This would never be allowed in the nursery/preschool setting. Hopefully, as society grows in its understanding of dementia, regulation and services of care facilities will improve to acceptable standards.

Environmental safety was of particular concern to me. It had been many, many years since there was a baby in our family. There were collectibles and breakables throughout our home, which had to be relocated when my grandbaby began crawling. What I had not anticipated was that Frank could see and reach everything; and without cognitive abilities, that posed a risk. I had to make a lot of changes, both high and low! These same considerations and adjustments are needed in any environment where a demented person lives.

"The club" was beautifully decorated with lots of large framed, glassed wall hangings. The little people loved to take round pillows from the hallway sofas and "hide" them behind the pictures. I had a constant fear of the pictures falling and either hitting a resident and/or glass shattering and cutting someone. Non-glass art would have been safer.

Another safety concern was the presence of hall table decorations with plastic fruit. Bobby was constantly picking and eating the plastic fruits. My grandbaby would do the same thing. They needed to be moved and eventually were.

I point these matters out because we are not used to thinking this way when dealing with the environment of adults. I certainly was not. We all make mistakes; what is important is that we learn and grow from them and prevent future occurrences, to protect our little loved ones. With better education about dementia diseases, with proper funding and regulation, and with committed staff personnel, the level of care will improve, similar to the history of children's day care facilities. It has to, for the sake of the little people.

May all those who work in dementia care facilities be graced with vision of the heart to tenderly care for these special little people, as they would like to be cared for when they grow old and helpless themselves.

CHAPTER

FOURTEEN

♥♥

…AS THE TREE

Father, I love you
And thank you for my life
Strengthen me to trust in you
Through struggle and strife
To follow the winding path
To follow the light
With faith and hope
In your promise, Lord
That day will follow night.

And He said, "My child,
See the tree
Giving all that it has
To the autumn earth
Standing tall
Through the winter
Awaiting spring's birth
Always to serve Me
Always to glorify My will
Oh, pray child
To be as the tree."

©Ellen Marie Edmonds 2008

Chapter 14: The Angel Miss Mawbley

The tree...giving all that it has...standing tall through the winter...awaiting spring's birth. What hope-filled obedience to God's will! And to be sure, springtime was coming.

Early into "the club" experience, I met a lovely lady who Frank called "Miss Mawbley" who worked at a bank during the day; and at night, she spent three hours at "the club" caring for an elderly lady who had all her mental faculties but was physically frail. Frank had always liked Miss Mawbley because she was nice to him, always smiling, dressed nicely, and was quite attractive! He called her a "classy lady." She had a special gift of kindness. In addition to all those reasons, I liked Miss Mawbley because of her special gift of caring for the sick and elderly. She had no children of her own, yet she beautifully mothered little people.

Miss Mawbley and I would often meet in the parking lot at night as we were going home. She had graciously found a daytime sitter for Frank, and Miss Mawbley herself agreed to stay with him on weekends. I planned to stay with him at night. One night, when Frank had become so physically diminished, I burst into tears of despair. Miss Mawbley asked, "Have you thought about bringing Frank home and hiring a live-in sitter?"

The next day, hospice suggested the same thing. Initially, a real fear came over me that I might not be able to meet his needs. However, hospice assured me that because I was so involved in his daily care already, I could do it. The day sitter agreed to move in with me; Miss Mawbley agreed to come on weekends; and with love and teamwork, we rescued my boy. The rest of that story is described in the next chapter, "Home Again!"

CHAPTER
FIFTEEN
♥♥

HOTEL HEART

Come on in -
There's always room for you
The light is always on
And me, too
There's lots of love and joy
Inside this place
And if we're still
We might just hear His face
And see His hug and feel His voice
Here - Inside His space
Mama warms the beads
By candle light
She sings her lullaby
All through the night
And softly shines her light
Through moving clouds
That cast their dancing shadows
On the wall
Until we see the promised
Morning call
Can you smell the teapot,
Whistling on the stove?
Can you hear the feathers' highest note?
Do you see the hopeful dance
Of the choral cats?
Ah! Life begins anew
At Hotel Heart
So come on in
And sing your song with me.

©Ellen Marie Edmonds 2008

Chapter 15: Home Again!

Frank used to say he had a "bounce to his gait and a jingle in his heart." Well, it was certainly with us all on that red letter day – Frank was coming home! Cats and the babe, flowers all in bloom... all of us wrapped in the warm glow of happiness, and singing our welcome home tune...

Fortunately, the basement of our home was finished into a large guest apartment. Al's widow, Barbara helped me get an extra bed for the sitter. Our friend Denny "Frank-proofed" the doors and added handicap rails in the bathroom. A new refrigerator, washer and dryer were added for the sitter's use. There was now a safe place for Frank to live, in his own home, in familiar surroundings - a factor important to dementia patients. I tried keeping him by myself on Friday nights, but I didn't have the strength. So Miss Mawbley covered the entire weekend, and life seemed normal again.

Frank was so, so happy! He began eating everything he could and regained 25 pounds quickly. Medicines were changed; continence returned. We took him out to restaurants often, something we had always enjoyed doing together. The sitters seemed happy, the baby was happy, and I was happy. Thank you, Lord, for making it possible to bring Frank home.

After a few months, hospice was about to release Frank from their program when suddenly, on New Year's morning while I was at Mass, he experienced a severe seizure and/or a stroke which left him unable to sit, stand, or walk without pain. Hospital tests could find no fractures. It appeared to be neurological. He was not a candidate for surgery.

From that day forward, with the exception of a few attempts at a geri-chair or standing up, Frank's life was spent between the rails of a hospital bed. We accepted this new reality and made the necessary adjustments to give Frank the best possible care. His bed was in the center of the room facing the large San Damiano crucifix he had given me years ago. Below was the television, and nearby was the stereo. To the right was an image of Our Lady of Guadalupe. On the left wall above the piano hung his prized sketch of a Native American bearing some of Frank's own Cherokee facial features. The artist, Frank's grandson David Ward Edmonds, had gifted Frank with this unique art treasure for his 70th birthday. He proudly showed it to all his visitors, always bragging about his grandson.

Frank never again missed a meal, or a bath, or a hug, or a kiss, a smile, a word of love. He was never alone again.   No one will ever know how important it was to me to be able to go to sleep at night knowing that my husband was home, safe and sound.   To be able to be with him *any* time was a grace, and I will always be grateful to our providential God.

CHAPTER
SIXTEEN

♥♥

YOU

Smiling blues on a Redskin – rare
Swelling hearts locked in stare
Kindness, endless, perfect pair
Happy always, anywhere
With you

A man's man, my armored knight
Crowned me queen, to keep you'd fight
Though oft you won by gentle heart
And knowing soul that cannot part
From you

Dearest friend, great wisdom missed
Grateful lips, daily kissed
Silent hugs – I hear them now
Purest Love; He shows me how
Through you

Memories cherished
Love lives on
Graced by Heaven's
Each new dawn
With you

©Ellen Marie Edmonds 2008

Chapter 16: Hospice and Hope

Through love songs and poems, the free heart gives light to darkness. Tiny bits of joy: blue eyes – opened; a new dawn – together. With God and hospice by our side those last 18 months, I was free to hope and to share the sacredness of every precious moment we had left.

Enough credit can never be given to hospice and the service it provides. In addition to the direct care given to Frank's basic health care needs three times a week, his medical supplies, and his medicine needs, they became a part of our extended family. The chaplain visited frequently and the social worker called or visited often. The social worker was particularly helpful in guiding me through a thought process and reaching a conclusion that medical tests, due to the trauma they would bring Frank in the hospital setting, were not in Frank's best interest. I had to ask myself what difference it would have made to have test results. What could we do to change the fact that Frank was dying? The merciful thing to do, I realized, was to not subject him to any more change or trauma than was absolutely necessary to keep him happy and comfortable.

It was at the request of the chaplain, confirmed by my spiritual directors, that I wrote a comprehensive letter to all of Frank's children and grandchildren, and to my family, explaining in detail Frank's situation, his prognosis, and requesting that they visit him as often as they felt led. We *both* needed them, I said. It was important to me to know that everyone connected to Frank, whom he loved, be educated and given the opportunity in Frank's final days, to respond in their own unique way to

God's call to love Frank, and in response to the love and sacrifice Frank had given them in his healthy years. One of Frank's grandsons, who lived too far away to visit and had been out of the family loop for a while, had called to thank me for the letter and for sharing those details with him. It meant so much to him to be able to empathize with his grandfather, whom he loved dearly and who had always loved him without condition.

There are many hospice companies out there. The services provided are as varied as the staff allows for. Some have an extended volunteer family, which I have heard can be particularly helpful to the family. The hospice which I chose was quite new, and there were not as many services available as with more established units. Because I had live-in sitters, some of those amenities were not necessary. And I believe that because our hospice company was so young, it contributed to the sense of family that developed as we worked together to meet Frank's needs.

There was an underlying sense of security and peace that hospice gave me, on a day-to-day basis, knowing they would be there when I needed them, and in the present moment of that last day. And indeed, they were there with us. I am forever grateful to hospice for their gift.

CHAPTER
SEVENTEEN
♥♥

THE MATRIARCH'S GARDEN

Fly away with me to the Matriarch's Garden
Where the River of Love pours freely…
Every fork – each branch with vine and Dove
Making its mark to the Source

Where earth and rain, fire and air
Tenth Choir! Winged Flesh!
Chant the Way to the sojourner's dayspring
With their nets of woven hands and hearts
Like feathers soft and strong
Lifting me and you and all who care, who dare
To plunge the dark River and follow its wind
Follow its bends of Hope
Dimly lit, brightly lit, warmly lit
By the Fire of Love, the Eternal Flame
Who calls us each one to The Garden

The roses wink in buds of pink
The morn gives its glory in blue
Birds and cats, the black Lolak
The grass all aglow in its dew
As the Brant hugs "I love you"

And the Old Soul waits between the rails
Where he lives and loves and waits
And friend and foe and seed alike
Plant memories 'neath the gates of the Garden

Colorful hearts imperfectly lived
Bloom and fade – perfectly loved
In joy, in pain – with Son and rain
Journey on – perfectly loved.

And the Old Soul waits between the rails
He loves, he knows, he wails
As the old tree dies and the New One born
He loves, he grows, he sails
On waters that flow in the Garden.

©Ellen Marie Edmonds 2008

Chapter 17:   Living the Present Moment

What does your garden look like? Can you still see the sway of ancient trees, dotting the river banks?   And the budding roses, beneath the morrow's thorns – waiting for your caress? They laugh, they sing, they light the Way to the Lover's hidden garden, in the heart of the present moment...

Sometimes it was in the middle of the night. Sometimes it was early in the morning. Often, it was only ten minutes since the last time. But always, it was the present moment. There, always, was Frank, me, and our Lord - and often times baby Brantley.

In the world of dementia, I learned, there was no yesterday or tomorrow. Not even a later or tonight. There was only now. How beautifully simple this way of living is. In reality, it's all any of us ever has. All the rest are just thieves of energy and seeds of worry. The beauty of dementia is that every moment of love is as if it were the first and the only moment. Isn't that, after all, what love is - one eternal moment?

It was Father Palmer who introduced me to the spirituality of the present moment. I am forever grateful to him for that gift. In some of those present moments, Father Palmer would often play his Native American flute for Frank who was himself, Cherokee. Frank would smile, look up at me and say with gratitude, "He's a good man."

Every moment I was with Frank, I repeatedly spoke familiar words of love and praise, which he never grew tired of hearing. This is the beauty of the present moment – love is always with you. This reality of time and eternity, this truth about love in the infinite present moment, is a God-given joy to all of us that transcends even death. But how do we embrace this gift and live in the present moment while trying to survive the constant heart wrenching struggle of dementia? When we are facing the daily demands of advanced dementia and the reality of hospice – that our loved one's life is coming to an end – while our self, barely afloat in a sea of despair from our own broken heart, how do we find hope? How do we companion our loved one into eternal life? What matters most about yesterday, today, tomorrow? What must I do and how?

Remembering how overwhelmed and exhausted I was most of the time, juggling Frank's care with the duties of a grandmother and all the household affairs previously shared by two, I realize that many readers seeking help may not have time to read this entire book at one time. Recognizing this fact, and remembering the request of a hospice nurse for a "quick list" to help families dealing with late stage dementias, I have compiled the following section called "In A Nutshell" as a quick reference.

Know that all who are affected by dementias, especially the "little people" themselves, are dear to my heart. It is my desire that all who are given the opportunity to love and care for those with dementia will look beyond the adult exterior to the interior child and be transformed in love. It is the same love which enabled others to care for us when we were little; and we will all be little again.

In a Nutshell...

From personal experience, I know how physically, emotionally, and mentally overwhelming it can be caring for someone with advanced dementia and/or in the late stages of terminal disease such as with hospice care. Tending to the normal duties of life in the present moment often consumed all of my time, money, and energy leaving little time for anything else. We can survive it, or we can embrace it, recognizing in life the importance of death as being second only to birth. The "dash" - which forever connects those two life events for your loved one, is about to be born. And in spite of all the suffering and sacrifice endured by the patient, the family, and caregivers, knowing in advance that death is approaching can be a wonderful blessing to all.

"In a Nutshell..." is a summary of care tips from my own experience, and what I learned from others in similar situations. It is offered as a quick tool for those who cannot read the entire book at this time, to help them face and embrace the reality that a life is ending, to help one zero in on what matters most to the patient and those who love him; and to help realize the intimate connection to one's personal faith walk. Although my own personal faith walk is Christian, based on the Catholic faith, it is influenced by and connected to all humanity through the love of our God. The important element is to connect with God as He is known to us. Know that He is with you in this time of trial, and acknowledge your dependency on Him, His love, His wisdom, and His power. His very spirit will guide us in every moment, if we but ask. In writing the following, I do ask Him to guide me in writing, and to guide you in reading, that we may put first-

things-first in the order of eternal matters. May God's desired will be done in all of us as we care for His "little people" in their final hour.

1. **Prepare and equip yourself and family caregivers.** As I embraced the reality of caring for my husband at home, I began seeking the advice of experienced caregivers, including friends, sitters, nurses, physicians and clergy. A "to-do list" shaped up very quickly. Among the needed items were *lots* of washable and disposable waterproof bed pads, extra long hospital bed sheets, lightweight blankets, specialty bed pillows, plenty of hygiene and grooming products, a medicine organizer, a pill grinder, puddings and fruit sauces for ground meds, plenty of laundry supplies, etc. Safety issues included installing deadbolt locks on doors, handicap rails in the bathroom, removing throw rugs and other floor items which could cause tripping. For in-bed bathing, vinyl floor mats were placed below the bedsides to protect the floor and prevent slipping. In addition to hospice care, sitters were employed to assure 24-hour care. Recognizing that changes in one's finances can affect care choices, home care may be the only option. There is an art to caring for the bedridden patient's needs, and we can all learn those skills! Hiring a professional sitter to conduct "family training" sessions and to "coach" caregivers is an invaluable service. Even contracting with a sitter for "on-call" advice or back-up sitting provides tremendous relief to the family. One of my greatest fears was that something would happen to one of my sitters and I would not be able to care for my husband alone; but the fear was relieved by the assurance of a church member who promised that she and her daughter were

always available to help me. Do your homework; equip your care environment; train the family; and line up your team. You can do it!

2. **Pray!** Believe that God is with you, in all moments of life, and ask Him to guide your thoughts, your heart, your words, and your actions. Pray often, throughout each day. A simple, "Help!" or "Thank you" directed to God is a prayer. Talk to God as father; ask for His help. Tell Him how you feel. I could never have survived, much less embraced, our cross without knowing God was real, and that he was always with me and listening. Sometimes, when I was in a hurry I would drop something and have to stop and pick things up. In frustration, I would look up to heaven and say, "Could you please cut me some slack here?" I realize that all that happens is His will; but I also know He has a great sense of humor, and He loves it when we are at wit's end and call on Him for help. Yet sometimes, we might feel so overwhelmed that we can't even pray. In those times, I would offer my struggles and daily duties themselves to God as my prayer. We must also pray *for* and *with* our dying loved one. Quite often, even when they cannot talk, one with dementia can still sing and pray. And hearing is the last sense to go, so speak softly and close to the ear. Try it, see what works. **Keep God present in every moment.** If you are not a person of faith or are uncomfortable discussing these type matters with your loved one, ask someone to help you. Maybe someone you or your loved one is close to has a particular gift for ministering to the sick and dying. My dear friend Dawn is especially drawn to these situations, and she was a God-send to us and to many, many other suffering families.

3. **Consider your loved one's faith walk and death requests.** If your loved one has particular desires or needs with regard to end of life matters, see to it that they are fulfilled if possible. For example, people of Catholic faith might desire the sacrament of Reconciliation (confession) and Anointing of the Sick, and wish to see a priest. People of other faiths may request specific faith or cultural traditions which should be honored if possible. There may be particular rituals and ceremonies, such as a Requiem Mass in a church or simply a memorial service for the family, which need to be arranged. Churches and funeral homes have staff available to help with these matters. There may have been a request for cremation or a clear opposition to it. Try to honor the wishes of your loved one if at all possible, so there are no regrets later. If these matters were never discussed beforehand, ask other family member or friends who love him and know him well to help you make decisions. **Do the best you can with what you have to work with,** and be at peace with your action.

4. **Forgiveness.** Every relationship incurs difficulties and painful wounds. Many are broken, with no communication for years. There may have been abuse, or infidelity, or irreversible harm. Whatever the case, there is nothing that God will not forgive of a repentant soul. But He tells us He will only forgive us if we forgive others. This truth is explicit in Matthew 6: 14-15 (NRSV), "For if you forgive others their trespasses, your heavenly Father will also forgive you; but if you do not forgive others, neither will your Father forgive your trespasses." Don't waste another moment playing host to unforgiveness; it is simply not worth the risk. *For*giving is the most

necessary form of giving - and it is essential to eternal happiness. From the words of God Himself, we must give it to get it. If you are having trouble forgiving your loved one who is dying, ask God and/or a minister or friend to help you. It has been said that a fine line separates good from evil in *every* heart. We all fail, we all sin, and we all need forgiveness and second chances. God created us perfectly imperfect! Seek to remember the good in this weak and little person, as in yourself. Forgive the bad in this weak and little person, and in yourself. Ask him to forgive you; tell him you forgive him. Even if there seems to be no response, gently speak the words. Let God do the rest. Make peace with your loved one while you can.

5. **Tell them you love them.** Love is a gift from God, who loves all of us: the good, the bad, the ugly. This is a time to focus on interior matters of the heart. Tell her why you love her. Thank him for the many ways he has loved you. The people we know and love in life are a permanent part of who we are. Recognize this, and express gratitude. Give these most precious words of kindness to your dying loved one. If there is resistance, let it go; God will honor your heart and your gift of love. Each soul is accountable before God; you will be at peace knowing that you did the right thing. And with dementia, it is possible for your loved one to respond with "I love you, too" straight from the heart, but without words. My husband was able to tell me those precious words with his eyes, a kiss, or just the beat of his heart. Say the words to them, and then listen with your heart... **Love transcends death; your hearts will be joined forever.**

6. **Love _yourself_.** Caring for someone who is terminally ill, especially when it involves dementia where the "person" has been dying little by little, takes its toll on the body, mind, and spirit. You may find yourself exhausted, acting out, or feeling out of sorts. It is important to love yourself! What does that mean? It means taking care of your own basic needs. If possible, take a short retreat to get refreshed. Go to the movies – I even ate the popcorn! Try to eat healthy, frequent small meals. Stay hydrated with water and juices. Take whatever medicines or supplements you need. Get plenty of rest and plenty of exercise. There is a tendency to develop a build up of stress hormones, which is lessened by exercise and by frequent deep breathing and slow exhaling to oxygenate your cells. Have a couple of friends who are willing to walk with you on this journey, and who will talk with you, eat with you, hug you, and be there for you whenever you need them. Many will run, but your true friends will be there.

7. **Expect the unexpected.** Family members respond to dementia and to death in ways never imagined. I witnessed a situation where four of five children vanished at the onset of their father's sickness, leaving the entire responsibility of the father's care, his death, and even his funeral to his wife and one child. I also knew of a highly respected prominent business man with a large number of children and grandchildren, whose funeral was attended by only two of his children. Who knows why children run from the call to love their parent when they are sick and dying, or to not honor a parent with their presence at the funeral. Perhaps there is unforgiveness, fear, pure selfishness, or some combination; whatever the case, be aware

that these situations do occur. Distilled to the essence, these are matters between the children and God, who tells us all to honor our parents, to care for them when they are old and demented, and that to do so is to atone for our own sin. He also tells us all that whatever we do – or do not do - to our sick and dying loved one, we are doing to God Himself (Matthew 25:45-46): "'Truly, I tell you, just as you did not do it to one of the least of these, you did not do it to me.' And these will go away into eternal punishment, but the righteous into eternal life." **Expect the unexpected, and do what you are called in love to do; give thanks for those who love and help you, forgive those who abandon and hurt you; pray for them, and leave the rest to God.**

8. **Journal.** It will be important after your loved one is gone, to remember those very tender moments of love, forgiveness, encouragement, last bequests, etc. A priest recommended that I use a journal as a form of grief therapy when my husband was dying. Gratefully, I also used my journal to write love letters to my husband and to record those precious moments of joy which became so rare. It has also helped me deal with feelings of regret or guilt. Since my husband's death, there have been times that I would involuntarily recall an experience from the early days of his dementia, when my responses to his new behaviors were uneducated and less than charitable... this was after his auto accident head injury, but prior to his diagnosis, and there were constant challenges and difficulties. When these memories pop up, I am always comforted by the entry in my journal of that sacred moment where we forgave each other for ALL the times we had ever hurt one another. It is a tremendous

consolation to me.   My journal became my best friend in grief, and it has been sort of a guardian angel of grief ever since.

9. **See the child inside.** With vascular dementia, the brain is going backwards to infancy. If you watch and embrace the journey - and keep a sense of humor - you may see in amazement behaviors for each stage of life in reverse! With my husband, I experienced this adventure as well as sporadic bursts of lucidity. Some moments held me in awe, some were funny, and some were embarrassing – just like with toddlers! What was important was my adjusting to who he was in the present moment. Sometimes he was Frank the man, sometimes the chatty or mischievous boy, sometimes the silent infant. As his able-bodied wife and primary caregiver, it was my job to adjust to meet his needs. Seeing him with my heart, he became my toddler and then my baby. In caring for my new grandbaby while also caring for Frank, I realized the parallels in their needs, behaviors, and my response. Once I embraced him as a child, the journey became much easier. He was a big child, like a toddler. He would respond to things with curiosity, the way a toddler would, and required constant supervision. Eventually, he became like an infant in bed, with the needs of an infant – though there were still lucid moments, knowing glances, and familiar kisses. A stuffed animal puppy gave him comfort and pleasure, as did the stuffed bunny to my grandbaby. Embrace the child inside, while respecting the adult you see, know, and love.

10. **Protect him from himself.** There was a story on the news of a gentleman believed to have had dementia, who ran through a street barricade, and ran over 50 people, killing a number of them. The

man was in his 80's. I wondered whether there was anyone who knew he should not have been driving. My heart was saddened by the thought that this man had probably contributed to society in many positive ways during his lifetime, yet he would be remembered for this tragic event which he may not even know happened. I wondered if he went to prison or to or a nursing home. That tragic event convinced me that I would have to protect my husband from *himself.* He was a wonderful man who contributed tremendously to society; how tragic if he hurt someone because his brain failed him! Fortunately, I took my husband's car keys, told him I would drive him wherever we wanted to go, and he never tried to drive again. Other areas of protection include financial matters, phone solicitation, legal documents needed for continued care, medical and geriatric issues. On the home front, it is also necessary to make the environment safe as you would for a crawling and walking toddler. If they can reach it or it can hurt them, move it. This caught me off guard once when my 6'4" husband reached up to pull something off a shelf that even I could not reach, and suddenly books came tumbling down upon him! His cognitive abilities were gone; there was no sequential reasoning. I had to look high and low to make his environment safe, had to use deadbolt locks to keep him from wandering outside or upstairs, and put in safety rails in his bathroom. These are just a few ideas about protection. Ultimately, the need is unique to each patient with dementia. The key is to make their world safe.

11. **Be kind and compassionate.** Think of the situation from the perspective of your loved one. If you had only a short time left, what

would matter to you? If you were confined to bed, your whole world was between two rails, what would bring you joy? Gentle words of praise and gratitude are always welcome. Favorite foods and treats; music and perhaps "dancing" will bring pleasure. Frank would often "jitterbug" in bed, moving his feet and shoulders to the beat of the music. It was one of the little joys that became big, because we could do it together. Assuring the person that you are with him and that you love him, even by a gentle touch to the hand, provides encouragement and a sense of security. If they say something which hurts your feelings, or if they fail to respond with words of kindness or love, accept it in love. When your loved one is gone, you will find peace in knowing you were kind even during difficult times. On the contrary, you may realize later just how sick your loved one was and gain a new understanding of why he behaved in a difficult way; and then you may find yourself experiencing feelings of guilt because of how you did or did not respond. Kindness always works and a smile brings comfort; if not to the receiver, at least to the giver. There is no need to argue, to be right, or to win. When in the gift of love you have chosen to let the other win, you have also won.

12. **Learn from your mistakes**. Everyone makes mistakes. It means you are doing something! Do the best you can with what you have to work with; and later, teach others what you have learned.

13. **Touch and speak to your loved one often**. If possible, give hugs! Hugs are therapeutic for the giver and the receiver.

14. **Give your loved one permission to go.** My husband had in-home care and had been bedridden for nearly a year when it occurred to me that he loved me so much, he would probably lay there in that

bed forever if he thought he needed to do it for me. He loved me just that much. Even though I had already made military funeral arrangements at Arlington and at our church, I had not consciously thought about a world without my husband in it. I just kept adjusting to each new day, loving him where he was. But as I was getting ready for bed one night, I pondered whether he might be suffering for me. For the first time, I thought about all the changes that would occur if he died. I would be a widow. There would be all sorts of unknowns to deal with. It was frightening to imagine. Yet, I knew at that moment I had to let him know it was okay to go if God was calling him home, no matter the impact on me. Then, if he suffered on for years and years, it would not be because I did not give him permission to go. Right then, I took my journal and I wrote him the most painful, love-filled letter telling him it was okay. It was our life story, as in the beginning of this book, but it was much more. I thanked him for the ways he had exceeded all his promises to love and care for me when he asked me to marry him. With great detail, I shared with him how lovely our life together had been, how grateful I was, and how now he was even taking care of my eternal life by letting me love him in his littleness. And then I told him it was okay to go, that we would be fine, and that our hearts would always be united in eternal love. All of these things I wrote to him in my journal; but still, I had not digested them. For two weeks, I reread my words, until little by little I began to accept that I had to let him go. Finally, on Thanksgiving weekend when he was suffering a brutal respiratory virus, I slowly read our story to him and gave him permission to go. Had I tried to do this earlier, I'm sure I would have sobbed and sobbed, which may have made it more difficult for him. But as it was, my heart had time to prepare so that I could be strong for him at the right time. Frank passed away three weeks later. **Letting them go is a necessary gift of love.**

15.**Prepare yourself to companion your loved one through death.** I remember how difficult it was to listen to my husband's labored breathing during those last couple of days. I had never been with anyone when they died. Hospice had not told me he was dying, I did not know how long the struggled breathing might last, and it was almost unbearable for me. My motherly instincts made me want to "make it better", so I kept calling hospice and doctors with concern. But soon hospice determined he was in fact approaching the end, and a priest with hospice experience graciously gave me a pamphlet which explained the symptoms and eased my concerns. I learned that the breathing was the body's way of preparing all the organs for death, and that it bothered me more than it did my husband. This fact gave me tremendous relief, and I was then able to cheerleader him to his goal of eternal life.   And within half an hour of learning that he would likely pass to eternity that day, my daughter called to tell me she was pregnant... Every ending has a new beginning. This alpha/omega gift from God seems to occur quite often.   As I began celebrating with Frank that his struggle was almost over, and that he was about to get his "doctorate degree in life" I also telephoned loved ones who were not present, so that those voices and goodbyes might comfort him; and perhaps it would give them peace later. This "end ritual" is unique for every person. If your loved one is in the hospital or on hospice, ask the doctor to have necessary medical orders on file.

Ask a nurse or the doctor for a pamphlet or guidelines to help you understand the signs and symptoms your loved one is experiencing. Consider what is best for your loved one and try to make it happen.

16. **Live in the present moment.** No matter whether your loved one is in an earlier stage of dementia, or the last stages of life, constant change can be a reality. Attempts to discern "the stage" were often frustrating, especially with vascular dementia, where there continued to be lucid moments. What worked best for me was zooming in at the present moment to see what would give my husband joy in that moment of "now", staying focused on his immediate need. Remembering that dementia is a disease of the brain, we can find comfort knowing that the heart does not get dementia. With your heart, you can communicate with your loved one's heart. Pray for God's help; even if you are not a believer, ask "God" to help you if He is *real*, and see what happens! God has a way of revealing Himself in dark moments. Count on His wisdom and mercy; know He is in the present moment with you. Through love and forgiveness, try to bring peace and inner healing to your loved one's life and your own. In your journal, capture these precious moments. Be gentle and kind always; with the eyes of your heart, see the little child within. Protect and nurture him; keep him safe. Hug and praise him often. Gift him with your smile. Listen to his heart beat. Walk with him, holding his hand, all the way to the finish line, trusting to hear God say, "Well done, good and faithful servant."

CHAPTER
EIGHTEEN

♥♥

RAILS OF LOVE

The beating of your heart still says
I love you
Words don't come, don't matter
To our souls
We kiss, we hug, we lay
Against the rails
That shape our world and
Share our every moment
Hoping for a glance that finds
The other's…
Eyes that smile our old
Familiar tune
Our song, our dance, our rite
Of all that is and was
And will forever be
So rare, so precious, ours
Gift of God to us
And us alone
Eternal flame that in the darkness peaks
And warms our world
Our life
Between the rails

©Ellen Marie Edmonds 2008

Chapter 18: Giving Joy, Finding Joy: New Ways to Celebrate

Living life between two rails has its challenges. But the upside was the discovery of new ways to celebrate our love and our life together, our gratefulness for one another, and all our blessings. That hospital bed, those rails, became "our place." Once, I even crawled up in the hospital bed with him, just to hug and hold him - and to get a glimpse of his tiny world view. Together, we discovered that it took very little to bring joy. In fact, as the darkness of night gives the candle its light, so the flame of our love brightened in our struggle through dementia.

Every morning began with a ritual. The day was filled with short phrases that he could feel and connect with. I would often bring his favorite meals from the restaurants we had frequented, hoping the flavors would connect him to joyful moments. He almost always had a smile on his face and a dance in his feet.

On our last anniversary, I asked the sitter to take some time away and let us celebrate alone. We had all our favorites - barbecue, chocolate pie. We watched a video of the last family reunion, and he connected with joy in the images of familiar faces, people he loved and missed. It was a beautiful moment for us.

Occasionally there were profound gifts of love, which I recorded in my journal. On one such occasion, I said, "Honey, I am sorry for all the times I may have hurt you. Will you forgive me?" Frank gave a resounding, "Yes!" "Thank you, Sweetie, " I said, "and I forgive you, too, although I can't remember anything you ever did to hurt me." And all was sealed with a hug.

There were also those moments where I missed and needed my husband - the man. I needed him to hold me. One morning, in a particular moment of weakness, I came to him in tears and said, "Honey, I need you to hold me. Will you hold me?" And with his "yes" he brought my head to his chest, and bringing his shoulder and chin together, gave me the most precious hug of my life. I was hugged; I was *hugged*!

Many moments like this were recorded in my journal, and bring me great joy and peace even now, when he is not here physically to hug. In reading and reflecting, I can embrace that aspect of the present moment and be blessed by remembering.

Frank loved his family, and especially babies. As the grandbabies and great grandbabies came along, I would surround him with large photos of them. Also around him were photos of his children and older grandchildren. So that he could see better, I used large photos. He would often hold the photos in his hands for long periods of time, proudly showing others and me his babies.

He also loved patriotic mementos of all kinds. There was always at least one American flag in the room – no proud soldier would be without one. These things gave him comfort and a sense of connecting to himself.

We continued the traditional rituals of holidays, complete with goodies. On his last birthday, just a few weeks before his death, I gave him just a sip of Jack Daniels on his tongue. Back in his younger days, "Black Jack" was his favorite. He licked his lips, sniffed a little, and then his eyes lit up. "Oh, yeah! I remember THAT!" he seemed to be saying. A Tennessee Squire could *never* forget old Jack!

To the end, Frank enjoyed football games on television, listening to big band music, jitterbug dancing in the bed, singing Christmas carols (any time of year was okay!), church hymns, and praying the Lord's Prayer.

Phone calls were a treat to him, and a gift from the caller. One of his daughters called regularly, which he enjoyed very much. A couple of his old work buddies called fairly often, too, and he would light up with joy.

I am forever grateful to those who made special sacrifices of love to bring joy to a man who could give nothing back, and whose life for a whole year was between two rails. May they be blessed as they have blessed.

CHAPTER
NINETEEN
♥♥

IT'S OKAY

…You have loved me so completely
So unconditionally
That I have experienced Heaven and holiness
In ordinary moments of life together
God has revealed Himself,
His Love and mercy for me,
Through you -
And I pray the same for you…
For I have never loved more completely.

Our friendship, our marriage, our love
So rare and so precious
Thank you for loving me
For letting me love you
In all ways
Especially now –
When you are …small and weak
I seek and find you
By the Great River of Love
That winds through the center of my being
I hold you, you hold me
Till death do us part
Yet, not even then
Two hearts forever joined
The eternal dance
That transcends pain and sorrow
Hearing only the melody
Of the mourning dove
I love you so much,
So much that my heart groans words -
Words that don't exist
Except in Heaven's Book -
And in the Matriarch's Garden

It's okay
I'll hold your hand, your heart
Along the way
We'll be fine, I promise. . .
Our love will only grow stronger
Day by day
In Heaven to stay
It's okay

©Ellen Marie Edmonds 2008

Chapter 19: Letting Go and Giving Permission

It was November 16th. Laying in bed that night, it occurred to me that Frank loved me so much he would lay there between the rails forever, if he *had* to in order to take care of *me*; and I loved him too much to let him. I had no idea what life would be like without him, but I knew I had to let him know it was okay for him to go if God was calling him home.

In my journal, I began to write our story. "He found me in the newspaper," was how it began. I reflected on all the ways he had loved me and the promises he had exceeded, what he meant to me and to my daughter, how he changed her life forever. The jewels of his love were sparkling radiantly from my heart as I wrote with deep passion. Towards the end, I told him that he had promised to take care of me for the rest of my life, and now he was taking care of my eternal life by letting me care for him when he could give nothing back. Finally, I told him it was okay - we would be fine. And we would be together eternally in God's love, our dance to the tune uniquely "us" would go on forever.

Well, it was written. But I could not bring myself to tell him these things just yet. But in a matter of days, at Thanksgiving time, he became sick with a brutal respiratory infection. Fearing it was pneumonia which could take his life, I got my journal and read it to him. It was a somber moment. It was the hardest, but the greatest gift of sacrificial love I had been called to give Frank. And in two weeks, it was his birthday - his last birthday - December 11th. Ten days later, Frank went home, with my permission and my love.

After Frank had died, the hospice nurse told me that Frank was only able to go because I *had* given him permission. My intuition had been right: he would have laid between those rails forever, if he thought he had to do it for me. That is how much he loved me. And I loved him so much that I could not let him do that for me. He had to know it was okay to leave, to be rid of his sick body, to go home to God. Death is the natural end to all life, and its sting the price of loving. And like taxes, there is no avoiding it.

Letting go and giving permission is a difficult, but necessary gift of love. Even for patients in a coma, hearing is the very last sense to go. The heart does not get dementia; they need our love to the very last heartbeat. And they need us to let them go.

CHAPTER
TWENTY
♥♥

DYING IN LOVE

From the moment of birth
Death begins
Slowly or suddenly
Surely
Sick, dying humans
Trying to live
Focused too much
On what's wrong, not what's right
Blinded by pride's dark night
Pride that itself
Is death's lead horse
And death to the horse
His Light
Holy Light, Holy Love
Holy Giver of Life
To all the sick and dying
Joy to the poor and crying
Hope to the failing and trying
In faith I know these truths
Source of all our hope
Given in Pure Love
Come to dwell among us
Because His Word was spoken
Hung upon the Tree
Because our love was broken
Forgiven in His rising
Forgiving broken love
Forgiving sick and dying
Creatures one and all
In hope who try, who fall
And in the darkest night
Are swaddled by the Light
Who hear His voice, His call
To follow in His love
To give and to forgive
Gift of life to death
Love of His own breath
Gift to all the dying
In Love

©Ellen Marie Edmonds 2008

Chapter 20: Frank's First Christmas

To die in Love is to live forever.

Sunday morning with his granddaughter had been so special for Frank, who was in a semi-coma by then. It was a gift of love, describing verbally her gift of photos he could not see; guitar playing; holding hands; covering him with his new red Christmas blanket...

Monday seemed to take Frank's breath away. Oxygen was administered for the first time, though seeming not to help. His body seemed to be shutting down, as the breathing changed. That same day, the weekday sitter left. Perhaps she was unable to accept losing Frank after 18 months of caring for him; perhaps the fear was death itself. My friend Lynn came to companion me, and agreed with me that he was dying, though hospice had not yet said so. We called hospice, and began praying the "Three Beautiful Prayers for a Dying Person" from the *Pieta* prayer book. Historically for me, within three days of having prayed the third prayer, our merciful God had often responded... Lynn spent the night, and hospice and the angel Miss Mawbley came the next morning. Barbara came, Father Palmer came, and a few other friends. After a hospice supervisor's evaluation, it was confirmed that Frank would likely go that day.

Thirty minutes later, my daughter Shayne called and announced she was pregnant. Omega with its Alpha, my now 2-year old grand daughter, Riley

Briel. The circles of life continue, blown as bubbles from the breath of God Himself!

Hospice ordered Frank's pain medication for this last part of his earthly journey, and I went to pick it up at a local drugstore. It was wintertime, and there were many customers waiting for prescriptions. What was probably only a few minutes seemed like forever. My mind and my heart were racing. Frank was *dying*! He needed me, I needed him, and here I was at a drugstore. "Excuse me!" I shouted to the pharmacist. "My husband is *dying* and he needs this prescription *now*! Can you please help me?" She was most graciously responsive, and I was grateful. Reflecting back, I wonder: how did my words affect those around me?

"My husband is dying." That was the first time I had said those words.

There was another medical item I had to get for Frank, and while waiting in the checkout line I looked around and thought, "No one knows that my husband is dying. I look like just another ordinary person on an ordinary day. But my husband is dying." That was a lesson in perspective for me. It made me realize that sometimes when I encounter a person, in a grocery store or other place, who seems to be difficult or impatient, perhaps someone they love is dying, too. Or maybe it is that person who is dying. No one knows the whole story. Kindness is always the appropriate response, for love is always kind.

Tuesday night, we were keeping vigil in prayer, with Father Palmer and Jesus in the Eucharist present for Frank's "graduation" from life. There was the hospice nurse, the sitter Miss Mawbley, Father Palmer, and me.

Wednesday morning announced itself with the midnight chime, and prayer continued. I went upstairs to get a special music CD for Frank when Andrea called me down. I had prayed to be with Frank at his moment and asked her to call me if there was a change.

His breathing was imperceptible, but his heart continued beating for about five minutes. During that time of passage, Jesus in the Eucharist lay on Frank's chest over his heart, and we called on Heaven to open its doors and receive Frank in mercy. Frank was about to get his Ph.D. of life, and I was trying to cheer him on and be strong for him.

And then - he was gone. The floodgates were loosed. Three years of tears burst forth in rivers, as I held my husband, my baby for the last time. "Well done, good and faithful servant."

And the rails were all alone.

Frank was a ham, and loved Christmas time. Having a holiday birthday, he would send reminder notices to family and friends saying, "I know that during this busy Christmas season, you would not want to forget the birthday of Frank Edmonds on December 11th." Sometimes the notice said, "There were two very important people born in December: Jesus Christ and Frank Edmonds." His sense of humor was contagious. Frank never wanted to be forgotten in the Christmas season. And as if prophetic, in the end, Heaven called Frank home at Christmas time.

He died in Love - and so he lives.

CHAPTER
TWENTY-ONE
♥♥

...Circles in the Wind

In Love we lived
Throughout your hour
Love so sweet
The l'emons can't sour
God's...
Circles in the Wind.

Lover and hero
Man and wife sixteen years
Love's joy and tears
Two who shared One Heart
Came death:
We did not part
Best friends...
Our Circle in the Wind

You lived – you gave
Path to Arlington paved
Living on after grave
Living on, living saved
Knowing...
Circles in the Wind

And the Wind breathes on
Tiny bubbles anew
Full of life and hope
Graced by memories of you
Alpha Omega
One and the Same
New sacred moment
Live on in His name
With you
Going on...
Circles in the Wind

And like a new bubble
I trust in the Wind
Oh, how shall He use me today?
With God as my pilot
And you in my heart
Leading on...
Circles in the Wind

©Ellen Marie Edmonds 2008

Chapter 21: Celebrating Death - Remembering Life

And the circles of life go on: living, loving, dying, and rising.

Frank saw death as the natural and successful completion of the Christian life, the Ph.D. He spoke often of Big Mama, of his late wife, and of Heavenly matters. He lived life to the fullest, and gave of himself to mankind in all ways. One of his greatest pleasures was living to see the birth of his first great grandson, an Edmonds boy who would carry the family name into a new generation and the new millennium. God had been good to Frank, to Frank and his late wife, to Frank and me, and to our children. These blessings we counted daily with gratitude.

We spoke freely and often about death. One of my fondest memories was Frank's dialogue with a fellow octogenarian. "If I had known I was going to live this long, I would have taken better care of myself!" Now Frank says, "If I had known Heaven was this great, I wouldn't have eaten so much oatmeal!" Indeed, he was a humorous man – a rare blend of humility and nobility - whose self-discipline and determination bore success.

Frank's birth into Eternal Life was his ultimate success. He was brave in life and brave in death, my hero of heroes. He was proud to have served his country as a WWII veteran, and later as a Civilian Aide to the Secretary of the Army for over 20 years. Even though Frank's career had been noteworthy as an officer of BellSouth/AT&T, in the end he was most proud of being a soldier. As a young man, he had been willing to make the ultimate military sacrifice for others, but was safely brought home by the God of Second Chances for a greater purpose: perhaps it was for the lives generated through the DNA of this man at the time of his death. Or perhaps it was the thousands of lives touched by his work. Only God knows the ripple effect of one soul, one life created.

In honor of his service to the United State of America, Frank had a full military funeral at our parish church, including a Visitation Service with the Rosary Prayer and the Divine Mercy Chaplet prayer. The inspirational eulogy delivered by the celebrant Father Palmer reflected on the unique story written with Frank's life. It was Christmas time, and those who loved him in sickness and in health were present to celebrate his life, his death, his love for us, and our love for him - all in the Christmas spirit.

Frank's life, and even his death, will be mystically remembered as a series of 21's. He was born in the 21st year, and died on the 21st day. There were 21 lives generated through his life at the time of his death. Honored with a patriotic burial at Arlington National Cemetery with its traditional 21-gun salute, he was proudly laid to rest in stack 21.

And so ends Chapter 21 of *Our Story.* ♥♥

After Word

Ellen Marie Edmonds

In Frank's *mental* death of dementia, I lost my husband, my soul mate, my protector, and my confidant, the man who was my best friend. In Frank's *physical* death, I lost my child - the man become baby. Each loss carried with it a grief all its own, forever marking my heart with love wounds, the jewels of the eternal crown. By the grace of God, I was transformed; and now life continues on.

For me, it was important to recall to my mind and my heart the joyful memories of "Frank Edmonds the man," remembering him as strong and wise and healthy; the man I loved and married, who loved me so beautifully, faithfully, and eternally. I needed to "refresh" my memories of "the man." The cherished truth is, I will forever know and love him as both man and babe; a truth, which, framed in God's love, is mysteriously Trinitarian.

The first year after Frank's death, I dedicated to rediscovering Frank - old videos, where I could see him and hear his voice, watch his gestures, and remember how he loved life and the people in it. The first December without him, I sent photo Christmas cards "Remembering Frank" and requesting the gift of a favorite memory of Frank on the enclosed card. The response was great! It was a healing end to that first year for all of us who love him.

But then it was time to remember me. The next year was dedicated to rediscovering "Ellen the girl, naked before God." Who was I then? Who am I now? What did I learn from this tremendous journey in the School of Love? What must I do now? How? When? Why?

As always, I started at the Source. During a 4 AM holy hour of adoration in the chapel at our parish church, I opened my heart and asked God to place in my heart the knowing and the desire of "next." I then wrote in my journal. It remains today a daily request, as each morning I consecrate myself to Him through the hearts of Jesus and Mary, asking to be filled with His Holy Spirit, to know and do His will in all my duties of life.

God's will. God's time. Our "yes." Could this be the perfect formula for a love-filled life, where "I" make love "live" in the world? I, you, each of us, with God's loving grace, can make a difference in the world. As Blessed Mother Teresa once noted, we are just pencils in the hand of God. What shall we write today, Lord?

It has been my privilege in the last year to lend support to a dear friend seeking physical and emotional healing through the twelve-step program of Alcoholics Anonymous. In this program, sick and hurting people help each other discover and rediscover the God who created us and loves us, and Who is omnipresent with us. As they listen and share their experiences of pain, others learn and grow. In that same spirit of hope for all of you who have just finished reading my story I say, "Thanks for letting me share."

STILL

It seems like only yesterday
That I could hold your hand
Your heart so strong
Beating our song
Still

Your sweet precious smiles
Twinkling blue eyes
Jitterbugs to my little tune
Holding hands
Then a kiss, kiss, kiss
Still

Soft gray curls
Longer than before
More of you to love, to hold
To let go…
To that place in time
In my heart
Where you are
Still

♥♥

©Ellen Marie Edmonds 2008

REFERENCES

Bereavement and Grief:

Community Grief Support Services, Birmingham, Alabama

Edmonds, Ellen and Hardy, Sharon Payne –
Finding the Path to My Second Wind: Restoring the Heart after Loss

Embracing Dementia: A Call to Love – www.embracingdementia.com

Hardy, Sharon Payne and Edmonds, Ellen –
Finding the Path to My Second Wind: Restoring the Heart after Loss

Lewis, C. S. – *A Grief Observed*

Neeld, Dr. Elizabeth Harper –
Seven Choices: Finding Daylight after Loss Shatters Your World

Wolfelt, Dr. Alan – *Living in the Shadow of the Ghosts of Grief*

Faith and Spiritual:

Baker, Bishop Robert J., and Groeschel, Father Benedict J., CFR -
When Did We See You, Lord?

Benedict XVI, Pope – *Deus Caritas Est (God Is Love)*

Catechism of the Catholic Church

Eternal Word Television Network (EWTN) – www.ewtn.com

Groeschel, Father Benedict J., CFR, and Baker, Bishop Robert J. -
When Did We See You, Lord?

Holy Bible, The – New Revised Standard Version (NRSV) Catholic Edition

John Paul II, Pope - *Rosarium Virginis Mariae*

Lewis, C. S. – *The Four Loves*

Pieta Prayer Book – *Three Beautiful Prayers for a Dying Person*

Shaughnessy, Father Angelus, O.F.M. Cap. - www.fatherangelus.com

Sixteen Documents of the Vatican Council –
Declaration on Religious Freedom

Solzhenitsyn, Alexander – *The Gulag Archipelago*

INDEX OF POEMS

As the Tree…	Chapter 12	162
…As the Tree	Chapter 14	186
B-r-o-k-e-n	Chapter 6	96
Chant to the Cherokee	Chapter 4	76
Circles in the Wind…	Chapter 1	26
…Circles in the Wind	Chapter 21	232
Dying in Love	Chapter 20	226
F-R-O-Z-E-N	Chapter 9	134
Golden Hearts	Chapter 5	84
Heart Tracks	Chapter 7	106
Healing Rain	Chapter 11	156
Hotel Heart	Chapter 15	190
It's Okay	Chapter 19	222
Jingle Bell Birthday	Chapter 10	148
Lily's Hope	Chapter 8	129
Love Lessons in the Rain	Chapter 13	166
Matriarch's Garden, The	Chapter 17	198
Mornin' Glory	Chapter 2	52
Morning Song	Chapter 3	68
Night Time	Chapter 9	136
One Dark Lenten Night	Chapter 8	128
Rails of Love	Chapter 18	216
Still	After Word	237
Transformed	Introduction	15
YOU	Chapter 16	194
Valentine Queen	Chapter 9	137
Widow Angels	Chapter 9	145

EMBRACING DEMENTIA
A Call to Love
♥♥

By Ellen Marie Edmonds

Regular Print Edition   -   ISBN: 978-0-9821984-1-4

Large Print Edition   -   ISBN: 978-0-9821984-0-7

Audio Edition   -   ISBN: 978-0-9821984-2-1

For additional copies of this book, check with your favorite local or on-line bookstore. If not available, please contact the publisher as follows:

DeetBrari LLC
5184 Caldwell Mill Road
Suite 204-255
Birmingham, AL 35244

Phone: 205 531-1813

www.embracingdementia.com
embracingdementia@bellsouth.net

thank you
♥♥